# Pub Walks
# in
# North Staffordshire

## Les Lumsdon and Chris Rushton

**Published by Sigma Leisure** – an imprint of
Sigma Press, 1 South Oak Lane, Wilmslow, Cheshire SK9 6AR, England.


**British Library Cataloguing in Publication Data**
A CIP record for this book is available from the British Library.


ISBN: 1-85058-316-1


**Typesetting and Design by:** Sigma Press, Wilmslow, Cheshire.

**Maps by:** Pam Upchurch

**Text photographs:** Chris Rushton

**Cover photograph:** The Black Lion, Consall Forge (Chris Rushton)

**Printed and Bound by**
Manchester Free Press, Unit E3, Longford Trading Estate, Thomas Street, Stretford, Manchester M32 0JT.  Telephone 061 864 4540

General Disclaimer

Whilst every effort has been made to ensure that the information given in this book is correct, neither the publisher nor the author accept any responsibility for any inaccuracy.

# Foreword

I've always been ambivalent about publications on walking. As a rambler myself, I tend to cherish the peace and solitude of a little-used by-way or bridle path and know that telling the world about it may destroy its very attraction. On the other hand, being furtive about a favourite walk not only seems selfish, it can remain so big a secret that the next time you set out for your blissful glade you find it has been ploughed away.

Fortunately there is little chance of that happening to those who are guided by the Evening Sentinel's popular 'Rambles' column. Shortly after I introduced the feature I took a telephone call from a reader who 'wanted to talk about the new walking page'. What I thought was going to be a compliment turned out to be a 15 minute complaint by a villager in the Staffordshire Moorlands who couldn't get out of her drive at weekends because Sentinel readers were using her road as a starting point to their walk.

So on behalf of that perhaps still housebound lady and all others who may be threatened by what I am sure, with this publication, will be a renaissance of rambling in Staffordshire, please be considerate for their peace and privacy.

*Sean Dooley*
*Editor, Evening Sentinel*

# To All our Readers . . .

Following the success of our rambling series in the Evening Sentinel, we've decided to bring together our experience to produce this attractive and timely book. There are thirty walks in all, visiting all of our regular patches, and some that we've not shared with our readers up to now. Not only do they capture the variety and interest of North Staffordshire, but they also feature some of the finest country pubs in our locality. What better way to start or finish a walk in the countryside?

*The Black Lion at Consall – a favourite of the authors*

We hope that you share our enthusiasm – and that of the Evening Sentinel's editor – for this is intended to be an introduction to the pleasures of walking in North Staffordshire's countryside. And do remember that it's almost always possible to get to our walks on local buses, so Sean's fears about housebound villagers hemmed in by our readers' cars are probably groundless!

It is most unlikely that you will encounter any problems but, if you do, please write to us via the publisher. Equally, we'd love to hear from you when you've enjoyed a Pub Walk in North Staffordshire!

*Les Lumsdon and Chris Rushton*

# CONTENTS

## INTRODUCTION

## THE WALKS AND THE PUBS

# Location Map

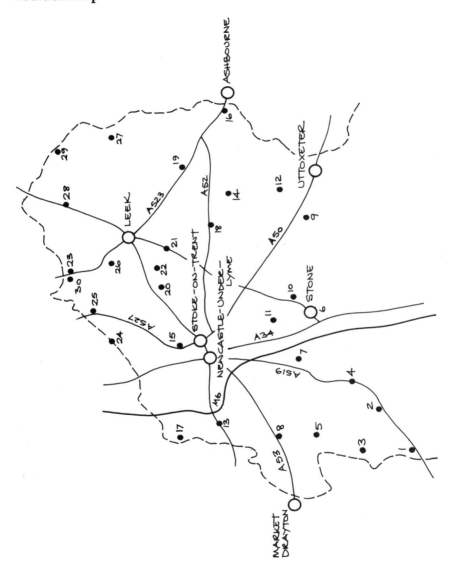

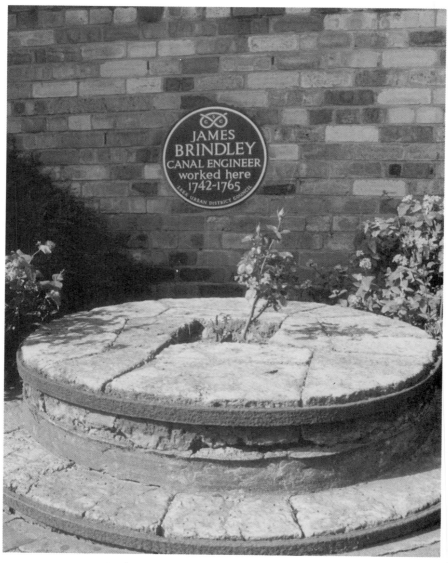

*Tribute to James Brindley, canal engineer.*
*This can be seen at Brindley Mill, Leek, on Walk 23.*

# NORTH STAFFORDSHIRE

Staffordshire is probably the least well-known of the mid-England counties. This is a pity for, within relatively short travel times, it is possible to walk the high ground of the Staffordshire Moorlands or through the gently-undulating pastures of western Staffordshire where damsons and sloe, hip and haw are still to be found in hedgerows.

## Richness and variety

The County has a richness and variety which tend to be overlooked by the would be walker. The thirty walks in this book, for example, make time for visits to parks and gardens, tread gently into the solemnity of parish churchyards and walk through past fortunes of villages and country towns. Several of the rambles invite you to wander by tranquil waterways conceived to fuel industry and almost all take you to pastures which have been farmed by local families throughout the ages. Beyond the towns, Staffordshire is still very much the latter-day rural England. It's all there: battlegrounds, stately homes, winding lanes in rich rolling countryside. Most of all, it is host to many a fine village pub.

The term 'North Staffordshire' is used liberally here to include the area surrounding The Potteries, the western fringes bordering Shropshire and the Staffordshire Moorlands stretching into the Peak District. This approximates to an area north of an imaginary line through the county town of Stafford (as a sister publication will cover the southern part).

Learned scholars have suggested that the county might well be sub divided into six parts in terms of landscape, three of which encapsulate North Staffordshire and it is worth pausing awhile to reflect on these. The Northern upland comprises the foothills around the Potteries, the edges and valleys which reach into the Staffordshire Moorlands. The higher gritstone ground of South Pennine ridges which surround the lower lying limestone pastures of the Peak National Park make the second component. Thirdly, North Staffordshire encompasses part of the central lowland, a lusher region characterised by dairy and cereal farming but undulating in parts to give that lift to a walk.

## 'Fruitful, Woody and Pleasant'

The landscape is drained by rivers flowing south eastwards, three tributaries of the River Trent. The book features walks in the valleys of the Blithe, Churnet, Dove, and Sow as well the wider reaches of the Vale of Trent. The lands surrounding these waters have aptly been described by Camden in 1586 as "fruitful, woody and pleasant".

The landscape of North Staffordshire strongly reflects its underlying rock structure. The upland area is carboniferous limestone, capped by gritstones, particularly millstone grit which has been used for walling, milling and some building. Newer red sandstones are also a feature especially to be noted in the Biddulph and Hollington rambles where the stone has been quarried for building purposes, evidenced in churches and large homesteads of the locality. The lowlands are dominated by marls, clays and gravels, the latter being deposited during post-glacial periods, thousands of years ago.

## Urbanisation

The urbanisation of North Staffordshire reflects the use of underlying coal seams, and clays. The growth of the ceramics business sector, dozens of china manufacturers within The Potteries, relied heavily on these raw materials. People tend to forget the uniqueness of this manufacturing base which attracts visitors from throughout the world. The ramble from Longport to Stoke-on-Trent along the Trent and Mersey Canal brings to life this historic legacy.

## Forests

Humans have moulded the rural landscape too. The walled enclosures of the Staffordshire Moorlands, the thickly set ancient hedgerows of the

Sow valley, the harnessing of watercourses can be attributed to human endeavour. The constant flow of changes, introduced mainly for economic gain, but sometimes for conservation or aesthetic reasons has been relentless. The Romans built roads through the area to the wilder parts of Wales and The North, and established fortresses to control their territory. So did the Normans and the remains of castles are to be found throughout the area. The powerful medieval lords built their power bases on the ownership of land. Therefore, the survival of forests as hunting preserves for the nobility, such as those at Needwood and another in North Staffordshire known as the New Forest. It is evident, however, that enclosures began to eat into these large tracts of woodland well before the forests were felled for charcoal and building in later centuries.

The enclosing of lands throughout the past three centuries has, until recent times, made the greatest impact on the landscape. The different shapes and sizes of fields, the planting of hedgerows and laying of walls, the building of tracks between village and fields, mill and maltster have endured a modern world. These early rights of way have been retained in law, if not always in use, so that those seeking access to the countryside can enjoy revitalised pathways for recreation.

In recent decades, field patterns have been broken up by modern farming methods, hedges grubbed and tracks removed. The economic pressure to farm large fields by mechanised means and with the use of chemical pesticides has had a considerable impact on parts of North Staffordshire. The Ordnance Survey Pathfinder maps often show field boundaries which have long since been grubbed and wet lands drained. The consequences for wildlife have, sometimes, been devastating. The work of organisations such as the Conservation Trust for Nature is admirable but their efforts cannot redress the balance completely. Fortunately, there are pockets of land where little has changed through the decades. These retreats offer rich reward to the walker and the authors have chosen paths in such areas wherever possible.

## A surprising area for walkers

Given the accessibility of such contrasting landscapes, it is surprising that much of the area is little walked. Not so long ago Staffordshire had a poor reputation for those who ventured out, armed with map, almost invariably found paths obstructed. The Staffordshire Moorlands and some parishes where locals have cherished their paths have been notable exceptions to the rule. The situation has improved considerably.

During recent years the County and District authorities have paid far more attention to the footpath network. Sometimes, waymarked routes and accompanying publicity information have begun to attract the potential casual walker back into local countryside rather than them travelling off to the Peak or Lake Districts. There is much more to do but at least the direction is now right.

## Ramblers

Let's not forget the enduring work of individuals and groups seeking to clear and maintain paths locally for our enjoyment. George Riley's work published in booklet form by the Borough of Newcastle-under-Lyme or those by Mr Brookes of Standon and the Eccleshall Rural Enterprise Group (routes are published in leaflet form by Stafford Borough Council) spring to mind as excellent local initiatives. Of national importance, in terms of campaigning for the walker, is the Ramblers' Association which has several local branches in Staffordshire who do sterling work to defend the rights of walkers. If you would like more information contact The Ramblers' Association at 1/5 Wandsworth Road, London SW8 2XX (Tel: 071 582 6878).

The authors first realised the extent of local interest in walking when preparing features for The Evening Sentinel in 1990. These features appear in the paper on alternate Saturdays. The appeal of visiting local villages, country parks and countryside locations stimulated far more 'phone calls and letters to the Editor than anyone had previously anticipated. These included enquiries about a book which would bring much of the material together. This text goes part way to meeting this request for it re-discovers locations visited in the Evening Sentinel articles, and introduces new walks in the quiet backwaters of North Staffordshire. Wherever possible the authors have attempted to avoid walks written up elsewhere.

No one is pretending that publicising local walks in this way is without some problems, particularly car congestion and parking hassles in local honeypot spots. This could apply to footpaths too, for there can be erosion or other damage. The Roaches, those mysterious craggy outcrops north of Leek, must be North Staffordshire's most celebrated example where walkers and climbers have saturated the area. The authors consider that by opening up lesser known places and by introducing measures to ease demand in sensitive areas matters can only improve.

## Pubs for walkers

A great joy of any walk (besides a good soak afterwards) is to adjourn to a local hostelry for a  pint of ale (or other beverage) either at the end of the day or at lunch. Inns have, throughout the centuries, welcomed the traveller on foot, farmers, miners and quarrymen going to or from their daily work as well as the coach traveller of the last century journeying across the land. Now, the country pub is geared far more to the leisure trade, although many still look after a local working population. Despite a dramatic change in clientele throughout recent decades, the tradition of hospitality and keeping good beer remains. Here, the authors thank The Campaign For Real Ale (CAMRA), which has, for the past two decades, championed the cause of the real ale drinker and the retention of characterful local pubs. Most will recall the work of the local branch of CAMRA in organising an excellent annual beer festival at The King's Hall, Stoke-on-Trent. The campaigning and social calendar of the group, however, continues throughout the year. Interested readers should contact CAMRA, 34 Alma Road, St Albans, Herts AL1 3BW (tel: 0727 67201) in the first instance.

There is a hitch, of course, for the rambler who loves real ale. Beer and driving do not mix at all. Every ramble in this book features a pub and several mention two or more *en route*. Those readers who find it impossible to pass a pub without sampling a glass or two, should let someone else do the driving. Better still, do as the authors did when researching this volume – use the local bus or train whenever possible. It helps to keep congestion down and puts money into a vital local facility.

# THE WALKS

The 30 walks vary in length from 3 to 8 miles and also in terms of effort required. They are, for the most part, easy going. There are a few golden rules.

Do not trust the weather. Always go prepared with a waterproof and a warm woollen. It might well be sunny when walking in the valley below but on the high Staffordshire moorlands the wind chill, even in summer, can be discomforting. In Winter it can be dangerous. The weather can turn wild so please be prepared. It is easy enough to take a light rucksack with the waterproofs and a light snack in case the walk takes longer than you first imagined.

The walks should be easy to follow by simply using a good map and the instructions in the book. There are two main problems regarding instructions for the reader. The first relates to how the authors perceive the route and describe it. They might consider a green lane to be the main feature and write this up accordingly. You might see the tractor tracks ahead as the way and therefore miss the intended route. If you do find yourself off the prescribed route, retrace your steps to a point where you found the text to be absolutely clear and then look again at the points mentioned by the authors to aid navigation. We quite expect you to curse us more than once!

## Things Change

The second point relates to when things change. As the countryside is a working environment field patterns, areas of woodland and buildings change. Please accept our apologies in advance for this. The text has been written so that even if a hedge is grubbed or a woodland felled, the way should still be easy to follow, despite the loss of an occasional landmark.

## The Pubs

Publicans in North Staffordshire usually welcome ramblers and all of those in this book have been approached by letter to ensure that details of opening times and the like are accurate at the time of writing, but our visits have been made anonymously.

Most country pubs in the land have changed in the past two to three decades to survive. The first major change is that most pubs serve food and this has become so important to their trading that publicans only allow people, ramblers or otherwise, to eat food bought on their premises. Most of the pubs in this book offer bar meals at lunch and in the evening but it is not usually the entire session, more likely to be noon until 2pm and from 7pm until 9 to 9.30 pm. Unless stated in the text the pub concerned does not allow eating your own (food that is) on the premises.

The same applies to muddy boots. Witness the increasing numbers of hastily written notes on pub doors "Hikers Welcome . . . Remove Your Boots!" Most pubs now have no bar with stone flagged or wooden floors where boots and wellies are accepted. Rooms tend to be carpeted. Thus, it makes sense to kick off your boots before entering to avoid the offence of being asked to do this. Sometimes, pubs have boot racks and storage areas in the porch for rucksacks.

## Families Welcome

The question of families in pubs often arises. Every publican in the book is happy to welcome families, especially if children are well behaved. Most have gardens or outdoor seats for summer use and this is ideal for the family group. Children are also welcome indoors if there is a separate area or room away from the bar. This a the law. Thus, it makes sense for mum or dad to simply pop a head around the door to ask whether it is all right bring the family in. Some hostelries feel they are not geared up for families every day of the week and say so.

The fortunate point is that many of North Staffordshire's pubs have not moved completely into the restaurant business but offer a warm friendly place to stop awhile and refresh oneself after a thirsty mile or two. The pubs are steeped in history and often reflect the locality they were built to serve. Long may they survive.

# 'Countrygoer' and public transport

The authors endorse whole-heartedly the Countrygoer concept, a campaign to encourage countryside lovers to leave their car at home whenever there is a bus or train alternative. This requires a little determination, pre-planning and a degree of ingenuity but it can add to the fun of the day. Some of the walks included are accessible by public transport every day of the week – Sundays too!

Useful contacts include:

**Staffordshire Busline:** run by Staffordshire County Council, and offering telephone advice for would-be bus and train travellers. Telephone: (0785) 223344

**British Rail:** (0782) 411411

**PMT:** (0782) 747000; the main bus operator in The Potteries.

**Baker's Coaches:** (0782) 522101; the company responsible for "The China Link' and other recreational services.

However you decide to travel, the authors hope that you have as much fun walking these routes as they had researching them. North Staffordshire offers much for the walker. Cherish it.

# 1. FORTON

**Route:** Forton – Aqualate Mere – Sutton – Fernhill – Forton

**Distance:** 6 miles

**Map:** O.S. Pathfinder 849 Hodnet and Norbury

**Start:** Forton Church (Grid Reference: 754212)

**Access:** There is a limited bus service from Newport and Stafford. Telephone Staffordshire Busline on (0785) 223344 for details.

*By Car* – Forton is on the A519 road between Eccleshall and Newport. There is limited parking on the road by the church, the first turning left after The Swan public house.

## The Red Lion, Sutton (0952) 811048

The Red Lion, a two roomed pub on the main road, is thought to be the only half-timbered building remaining in Sutton. It was not built as a public house, but most probably a farmstead in the village and was listed as such in 1895. A leaflet published by the Newport and District History Society suggests that, by 1925, it was shown as an inn supplied by the Newport (Salop) brewery, although the pub still had outbuildings for cows, horses and pigs. Like so many roadside inns in the last century, the incumbent was still involved in small scale farming.

The Red Lion is open from 11am until 3pm Mondays to Saturdays and from 7pm in the evening, although in the summer opening is closer to 6pm. Usual Sunday hours observed. Cask Conditioned Banks's Mild and Bitter are available and food is served at lunchtimes and early evenings until 9 pm. Families are welcome and there is an extensive garden and well kept play area.

# Forton

The hamlet of Forton stands around the pleasantly situated hillside church with its sturdy 13th century pinnacled tower and Georgian nave and chancel. Next door stands the handsome Forton Hall, a Jacobean style house dating from the 1660s.

*Jacobean-style Forton Hall*

Sutton, like Forton, grew up as a small agricultural community near a junction of roads. One such road was a roman link between the Whitchurch (in Shropshire) and Watling Street at Weston. The Aqualate Mere and park influenced the landowning pattern of the area too. Held by Earl Algar at the time of the Domesday Survey the wooded slopes leading to the mere were thought to be one of the earliest deer parks in the land. In later centuries a Jacobean hall was built in the park. This was embellished for Sir George Boughey in the early years of the 19th century, the work being undertaken by the famous John Nash. The equally-important landscape gardener, Humphrey Repton, worked on landscaping the parkland to blend in naturally with the surrounding countryside. Unfortunately the masterpiece of a house burnt down in 1910 but the park remains and is to many a mysterious place rich in wildlife.

# The Walk

(1) Start from the entrance gate to Forton Church. Turn left to walk down the hill. At the small gate go left to enter a field below the churchyard. The path follows the line of ancient oaks and then climbs along a green track to cross the line of the Newport Branch canal, opened in 1835 to link the Shropshire Union with the Shrewsbury Canal. It never really succeeded as a canal and fell into disuse in the 1940s. A section in water survives at Norbury Junction and another at Newport. Otherwise, the canal has been filled in or remains in a sad state as here.

(2) Once over the canal the track curves left to go through a gateway and ahead through another gate by a tree. Keep ahead to another opening and go over a ditch. Then, walk ahead again towards the far left corner of a field where you cross a stile and go through a small gate. Cut left and follow the hedge to a pool.

(3) Go right here along a track to cross a drainage ditch and head towards the wood on your left, Thistleyfield Covert. The atmosphere is eerie, low lying land with a stillness of air broken only by wildfowl rising from the mere hidden behind the trees. Once over the ditch, small pool to the left, proceed ahead through a field to cross a double stile near to bushes to the left of a protruding hedge. Bear slightly left towards the wood until wicket gate is reached by a wooden barred gate. Head slightly right towards the wood to the right now and look for a gate, usually tied with rope and wire. Go over another water channel and a narrow path leads into the wood, a path lined with bluebells in spring.

(4) The path soon forks. Keep to the left to approach another ditch, crossed on broken branches. It continues to wind its way ahead between young trees and offers a glimpse of the mere at this point. It runs ahead beneath a small bluff on the left and exits the wood by a stile into a

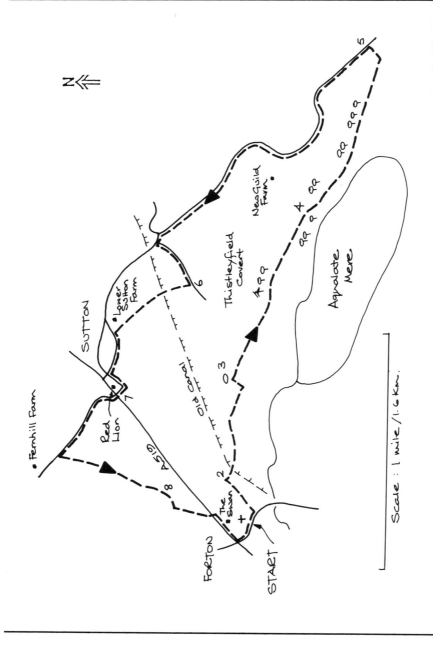

Scale : 1 mile / 1.6 Km.

pasture. Keep ahead along the wood's edge. Once through the next hedge go left to a gate and up a tractor track which becomes a hedged lane leading to the road. Turn left.

(5) This narrow road bends left and passes by New Guild farm on the left. It continues to a junction with a turning on the right to Gnosall. Just before the rise to the old canal, go through double gates on the left. The lane soon bears right and proceeds along another straight section.

(6) Go through a gateway and then turn right to walk up raised earthworks over the canal. Go through gates here (mind the barbed wire) and walk down a green track to go through another gateway. Continue ahead over a ditch and bear slightly right to ascend a large field with Sutton on the hillside to the left. In the far right-hand corner by Lower Sutton Farm go through a barred gate and onto the road. Turn left for Sutton village and The Red Lion along to the right.

(7) On the main road (having retraced your steps from the pub) turn next right to pass by houses and cottages to leave the village. The road rises between fields and then begins to curve right towards Fernhill Farm. Look for a gateway on the left between two small metal posts. These fields tend to be cropped but be assured that the right of way heads slightly left to join an extruding field corner. Keep ahead alongside the hedge. When this cuts left continue straight on through the field. It is difficult here for the original field boundaries have been grubbed and the path would have followed these. To the left is a conical shaped folly said to have been built in the 18th century as a truncated windmill,and is often mistaken as a small lime kiln of sorts.

(8) However, head for a point just to the left of a solitary oak in the middle of this large field. From here your landmark, the church tower, is now much clearer. Walk in the direction of the church towards the wooden fencing. Cross the fencing (a stile and signpost have been suggested). There should be a little link path through a gate on the other side of the road which leads to the bottom of the churchyard where the walk commenced. When researched it was extremely difficult to pass and the matter has been taken up accordingly. Meanwhile, turn right on the verge by the main A519 road. Walk by The Swan and then take the next left to the church.

# 2. WOODSEAVES

**Route:** Woodseaves – Hollow Farm – High Offley – The Anchor – Woodseaves

**Distance:** 4 miles

**Map:** O.S. Pathfinder 849 Hodnet and Norbury

**Start:** The Cock, Woodseaves (Grid Reference: 799254)

**Access:** There is a limited bus service on Mondays to Saturdays from Stafford. Contact Staffordshire Busline on (0782) 223344

*By car* – Travel on the A519 through Eccleshall. There is limited on street car parking on the B5405 or High Offley roads. Please park considerately.

## The Cock (0785) 284270

The Cock Inn at Woodseaves is an unspoilt pub in a village which amazingly sports three hostelries. The homely bar and lounge rooms are served from a central bar and there is a small restaurant room to the rear. The Cock serves a well kept pint of Banks's Mild and Bitter and provides food (which is mainly home made) throughout all sessions. A take-away service is offered too! The Cock is open all day from noon on weekdays and observes the usual Sunday opening. Families are welcome and there is a garden to the rear. The Cock offers a warm welcome to ramblers and makes for a good setting off point for this little adventure.

## The Anchor (0785) 284569

The Anchor must be one of the most unspoilt canal-side pubs in the country with its open fire and settles, ciders and beers dispensed from a small bar. It has changed little since the 1830s when it served bargees who sought to stable their horses overnight for a good rest. The pub stands near Bridge 42 and not far from the Grub Street Cutting which was bedevilled with landslips and breaches in the first years of operation. This activity was often the talking point of the entire pub for months on end. The pub was originally known as the New Inn and then in the 1850s changed name to the Sebastopol as a memorial to the Crimean War and only later became The Anchor.

*The Anchor*

The pub has two distinct seasons. In the Summer (Easter until the end of October) it is open on Mondays to Saturdays from 11 until 3pm and from 6pm in the evenings. On Sundays it is open from noon until 2pm and from 7 until 10.30pm in the evening. In the Winter, opening is limited to Thursday and Friday evenings, Saturdays as in Summer and Sunday lunch only. Wadworth 6X, Marstons Pedigree and the Winter brew Owd Rodger are available all year. The Anchor also has an extensive range of ciders including traditional beverages sold from polypins. Sandwiches are on offer and while families are welcome in the garden by the canal, children under 14 are not allowed in the pub as there is no separate room from the bar. So rest awhile in this traditional pub and reflect on what life might have been like for bargees a hundred years ago. The Owd Rodger will help to stimulate the imagination.

## Woodseaves

Woodseaves has always been a resting place for weary travellers on the A519 – a road known in previous centuries as the Portway. While most people now commute to work from the area, there is still an agricultural interest and the community sustains a village shop. For many centuries the villagers had to walk to High Offley church to worship. This church is seen throughout the walk, a sandstone building standing on high ground with the old school, pub and vicarage standing nearby.

# The Walk

(1) From the Cock Inn, turn left and then next left into High Offley Road. Follow the road out of the village to pass Home Farm then to Hollow Farm. Just beyond a traditional red brick barn the road comes to a house at a sharp bend.

*The Cock Inn, Woodseaves*

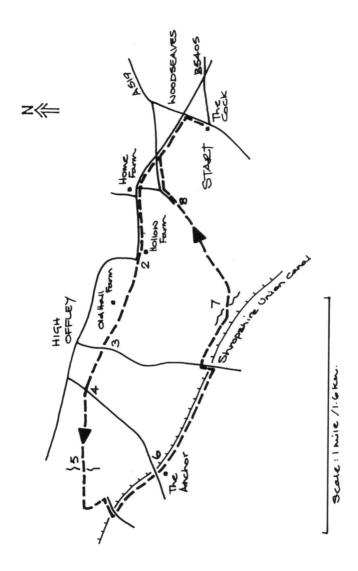

(2) The footpath to High Offley is signposted ahead through a gate. Then, go left to cross wooden fencing. Once over, turn right to follow the hedge to a gap which leads into the next field. Keep ahead to a kissing gate and then bear slightly right through a pasture with Old Hall Farm to the right. Cross a stile and continue straight on with the hedge now on your right. Cross another stile and keep ahead to a stile, not easily seen, which exits onto a narrow lane. Go right here for the church but otherwise your way is ahead.

(3) Cross the road and climb the steps up the bank to a field offering a good view to the old parsonage on the left and former schoolhouse on the right. Walk straight across the field to drop down to another road. Those seeking a shorter route will turn left here for a half mile bee line to The Anchor Inn.

(4) Otherwise, cross the road and stile and continue ahead through a low lying pasture. The path is not clear on the ground here but, before reaching the field corner, go right and left through a gateway (a pool is on the left and a bed of camomile lines the path). In the next large field head slightly right, towards the right-hand electricity pole. Drop down to the stream here and cross to the other side. At the time of writing the authors found the banks eroded and wire fencing making an ascent difficult so please take care here.

(5) Bear slightly right up the field towards a gateway beneath a young oak tree but do not go through. Turn left to follow the hedge until a gate at the corner. Go through this and up the track to the canal. Look for a stile at the far end of the bridge on the right. Drop down to the canal towpath and turn right under the bridge. The path leads to The Anchor.

(6) Suitably refreshed, continue ahead to the next bridge spanning a wooded cutting. A path leads up to the right of the bridge. Turn left and cross the bridge but, before the grass verge belonging to a  cottage on the left, look for a gap in the wood on the right and follow a well-worn path ahead. The wood is threaded with unofficial paths. Yours winds its way ahead, through rotting tree trunks and fungi, keeping closer to a ditch and fields on the left than the canal on the right. It climbs a slight bluff and you then look for a spur off to the left, down steps to a footbridge.

(7) Bear slightly right across the narrow enclosure. Cross a stile and go right along the field's edge to the top far corner. Cross a double stile here and bear slightly right to progress in a similar direction across a field often in cereal crop. Cross the fencing by a barred gate and keep ahead with a hedge to your left, to a stile by a gate with a barn and repair works to the left.

(8) Walk up the track to a road junction and turn right. This soon brings you to the High Offley Road where you turn right back into Woodseaves.

# 3. KNIGHTON

**Route:** Knighton – Offley Grove – Shebdon – Shropshire Union Canal – Hopsort – Knighton

**Distance:** 6 miles

**Map:** O.S. Pathfinder 849 Hodnet and Norbury

**Start:** Canal Bridge at Knighton (Grid Reference 747268)

**Access:** Knighton is very poorly served by bus. Check with Staffordshire Busline on (078) 223344.

*By Car* – Travel on the A519 to Woodseaves, then turn right for High Offley. Nearly a mile beyond turn left for Shebdon and then right for Adbaston, passing the Wharf Inn. Go left at Adbaston for Knighton by way of the Haberdashers Arms. There is limited on street parking near the Knighton factory.

## The Haberdashers (0785) 280339

The Haberdashers Arms stands on a small agricultural estate once owned by the Worshipful Company of Haberdashers (the word haberdasher meaning a dealer in articles of clothing). The rents from the estate were evidently partly devoted to the running of the Adams Grammar School in Newport in earlier times.

The Haberdashers is a traditional pub, with several rooms served by a small central bar. It serves the local community but is used to welcoming those cruising by on the nearby Shroppie canal, also the few ramblers who have come to know this area. Cask conditioned Banks's Mild and Bitter are on offer. Hot pies are sold but the publicans do not mind ramblers bringing their own sandwiches. Families are welcome and there is a pleasant garden which is ideal in the summer months.

The Haberdashers is rightly proud of its Potato Club (see the photographs on the walls) which encourages its members to grow prize potatoes for an annual show and competition at August Bank Holiday Weekend. At the meeting members must show six quality, six heavy and a single heavy potato before entering any other classes. It is a serious business! Opening times are 6.30pm in the evenings (no lunchtimes on Monday to Fridays), 12.30pm until 3pm on Saturdays and usual Sunday hours. This out-of-the-way hostelry is well worth a visit.

*The Haberdasher's Arms*

## The Wharf, Shebdon (0785) 285041

The Wharf, like The Haberdashers, is an isolated pub. It was built to serve the navvies working on the canal construction and for boat people throughout the subsequent decades. The pub is at road level as the canal is at a much higher elevation at this point. The name derives from Shebdon Wharf, where a crane and workshop still exist. The Wharf pub has a small bar where a variety of games are still played including the rare bar billiards. The modernised lounge has several areas and there is a restaurant.

The Wharf offers Tetley Bitter on hand-pull but perhaps more-interestingly has a rotation of two other cask beers. When the authors visited (for quality control purposes, of course) the pub was offering Brains SA (known to beer afficionados as Skull Attack) and Holts Entire (the HP&D Midlands brewery subsidiary of Allied Breweries rather than Holts of Manchester). Opening times are 6pm in the evenings, noon until 3pm on Saturdays. The Wharf opens weekday lunchtimes during the summer only. Food is served and families are welcome. There is a large outdoor garden area.

# Knighton

The Shropshire Union Canal linking the North West (Ellesmere Port) to the Midlands (near Wolverhampton) was probably the last rural mainline canal to be built in this country. What makes it so interesting is its deep cuttings, and high embankments such as the one featured in this ramble at Shebdon Wharf. Can you imagine how many navvies there would have been working on this section alone in the 1820s? It took a good ten years to open the canal fully to through traffic, mainly because of the technical difficulties in securing the embankments in western Staffordshire. Thus, by the time it was complete the railways were establishing at a rapid pace. Ten years on the canal became the property of the Shropshire Union Railways and Canal Company and within a further two or three years this was absorbed by the massive London, North Western Railway company, the LNWR. In fairness, to the latter organisation it allowed the management of the Shropshire Union to build business throughout the last century.

The Cadbury's factory at Knighton was a major user of the canal in the early decades of this century. This was originally a milk evaporation plant with the resulting product being added to the chocolate making process. Cadbury's owned a distinctive fleet of liveried boats which collected milk churns up and down the canal, transported "chocolate crumb", and other materials. They were all named Bournville (I, II, III etc) after the company headquarters. The fleet lasted until the late 1920s. Amazingly, chocolate crumb was still being despatched by boat to Bournville in 1960. The Knighton factory thrives to this day.

# The Walk

(1) From the entrance of the factory turn right to walk away from the canal on the road to Adbaston. The road descends a little then begins to bend to the right. Just beyond houses on the left, go left along a track which leads into fields and Knighton Grange, a good looking red brick farmhouse with unusual windows standing to the right. The track comes to a junction.

(2) Go right and follow the bridleway past the rear of Knighton Grange and around the corner to the left. A few paces on the bridleway bears right along a green track and you keep ahead along another track which curves right to cut the corner of the field, to the right of an old scar which is used for breeding pheasants now.

(3) Go through a gateway into a large field. Leave the track here which continues to The Drumble and is not a right of way. Instead, go ahead along the hedge on the left and by Knighton Wood where there has been some clearance work during recent years. The church seen ahead is at Cheswardine, the village which is said to hold the secret recipe of the aphrodisiac Gingerbread. At the end of the field, you come to a gateway. Go through it and walk down the bank through scrub. There is a view of the Knighton Reservoir here, built as a feeder to the Shroppie Canal. The path dips to the Waggs Brook. The boundary is difficult to cross here being a tangle of wire (a stile has been suggested).

(4) The brook also marks the boundary with Shropshire. Walk slightly right across the field in the shadow of the reservoir embankment. Follow the field edge up to an apology for a stile made of bits of wood and pig wire. Once over walk along the fence ahead to go through a gate. Turn left and follow the hedge to exit by the drive of a bungalow on the left. The gap, sometimes blocked up by wire is beneath the electric telegraph pole.

(5) Turn right to walk to the few houses at Hopshort. Bear left to walk along the lane to the bridge (No 48) over the Shropshire Union. Go left down to the towpath and proceed ahead for approximately one mile to the cutting at Knighton. The walk can be shortened by leaving the canal here. Otherwise continue ahead for a half mile extension along the

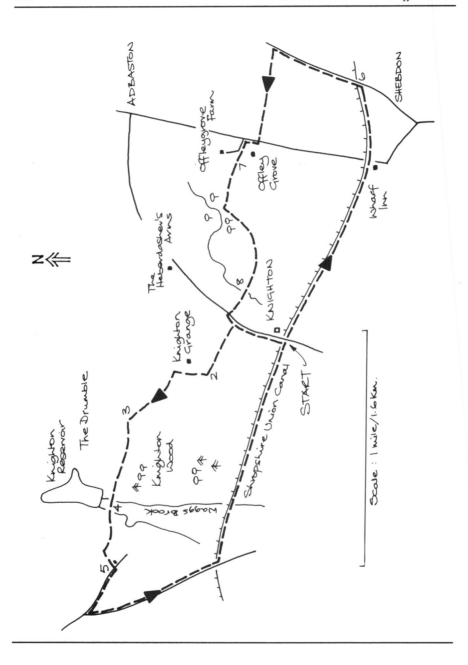

embankment to Shebdon Wharf. Opposite the wharf crane and building cut right down steps to The Wharf public house if stopping for refreshment. If not, continue to the next bridge at Shebdon.

(6) Climb up to the road and turn left to cross the bridge. At the first junction, go left along a bridleway to the entrance gates of Offley Grove. Turn right on the road but then take the next drive left to Offley Grove Farm, well known in recent years for its sheep rearing and production of cheese. Offley Grove Farm offers accommodation and camping.

(7) As the drive bears right to the farm keep ahead through a gate and along a tractor track which descends to a junction before the wooded stream ahead. Go left here and follow the track as it rises to a small piece of woodland on the left which hides a pool. The right of way continues ahead here across the field to a gateway, although the track, which some walkers use, follows the field hedge left and then right to another gap in the hedge. In the next field, go straight on to find a bridge (in a state of poor repair, so take care) over the brook, or you might like to use the gate and ford the water.

*The Shropshire Union Canal, near Knighton*

(8) On the other side the path leads around the right-hand bank of the fishing pool and then cuts right up the field to the corner of a garden. Walk ahead along the hedge to pass by a small building which looks as if it could once have been a smithy. The path exits onto the road. Turn right for the short stroll to the Haberdashers and left for Knighton factory.

# 4. ECCLESHALL

**Route:** Eccleshall – Smithy Lane – Copmere – Pershall – The Leys – Eccleshall

**Distance:** 5 miles

**Map:** O.S. Pathfinders 850 (Stafford), and 830 (Stone)

**Start:** Eccleshall Church (Grid reference 827292 )

**Access:** Eccleshall is served daily from Hanley and Stafford by bus. Contact Staffordshire Busline on (0785) 223344 for details.

*By Car* – Travel on the A519 to Eccleshall. There is a small car park on the B5026 road.

## The Star Inn, Copmere End (0785) 850279

The Star Inn is an attractive looking pub to be found at the bottom end of Cop Mere. Enjoyed by bird-watchers and fishing folk visiting the mere as well locals and ramblers, the Star has a country atmosphere lost in many pubs nowadays. This two roomed pub is also home to an old-established horticultural club which has a show of various vegetables and flowers every Sunday lunch, after which the produce is auctioned off in the pub! The Star is well known for other auctions where proceeds are donated to charities.

Open all day from noon during the week and usual Sunday hours, your hosts offer an exceptional pint of Draught Bass. Food is available from midday until 4pm and from 6pm until 9 pm. Families are welcome and there is a large garden and play area. Altogether, this is a friendly hostelry, with open fires in winter, and is deservedly popular with walkers.

*The Star Inn, Copmere*

## Eccleshall

Eccleshall is one of Staffordshire's delightful little towns which typifies rural life in mid-England. While it has become far more of a dormitory settlement in recent times the town maintains a local character which is steeped in history. Eccleshall has a group which continues to champion the cause of tourism in the area on a scale which is not obtrusive to the local community. As part of the Village Enterprise initiative a few years back a local butcher decided to create a new delicacy, The Eccleshall Pie, which can still be bought to this day in the High Street. There are also local Village Guides who are willing to show parties around the Eccleshall area and they do know every yarn about the place from celebrated marriages to macabre murders.

The large parish church is the resting place of several bishops for until the last century nearby Eccleshall Castle was the main residence of the Bishops of Lichfield. The castle is now closed to the public but the church is well worth a visit. A walk down the High Street in Eccleshall soon brings the walker to several old coaching inns because Eccleshall

*The Church, Eccleshall*

became an important coaching centre in the last two centuries and therefore has several legends associated with the transport trade. One such extract in "The Gentleman's Magazine" in 1807 recounts such a tale:

"Early in the morning the heavy Chester coach stopped at the house of T. Bagnall, at Eccleshall in Staffordshire, horsekeeper to the coach. The people perceiving neither coachman nor outside passengers, but those inside fast asleep, a search was immediately undertaken; when it appeared that the coachman had fallen from his box at Sughill, a distance of three miles from Eccleshall, and that the horses had instinctively drawn the coach to the door of the horse keeper's, which is about eighty yards from the inn. The coachman was found, quite dead, in the highway in his usual position of driving, and was neither bruised, nor apparently otherwise injured. He is supposed to have died suddenly on the box."

The phrase "falling off" to sleep comes from the halcyon days of coaching when passengers or drivers occasionally nodded off and literally fell off the coach in sleep! This must be a classic example.

# The Walk

1. Walk through the imposing lych-gate towards the parish church. Walk to the right of the church through the churchyard to a kissing gate. Once through, proceed ahead to a gateway at first then bear right across a well-worn and sometimes wet path across the meadow to exit on the main Newcastle road by the lodge to Eccleshall Castle.

2. Turn left and walk along the pavement by the road, over the bridge and around the sharp bend to the left. As the road veers right keep left along a track opposite a large walnut tree. Pass by a pool on the right and then look for a stile on the right at the corner. Go over this and head slightly left down a gap to cross a double stile into the next field. Head slightly left across this pasture to cross a stile with a warning that there may be bulls ahead. When the authors walked this path, the field was in crop with maize corn and not a bull in sight.

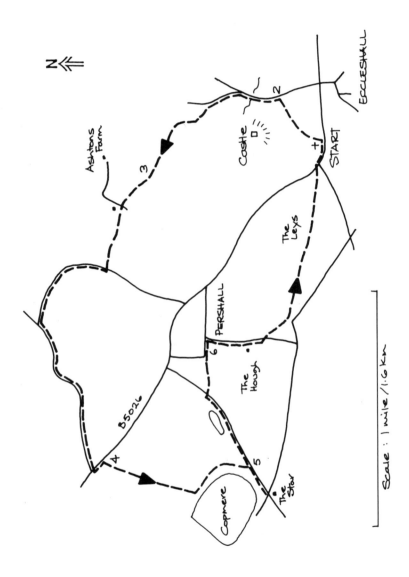

3. Go straight on to cross two stiles and a track, leading on the right to Ashtons Farm. Your way, however, is ahead along the track towards a little cottage in the distance. The path passes in front of the cottage and outbuildings to a wicket gate and then onto the drive. Follow this to Smithy lane where a right turn is made. The lane soon bears left and continues to a junction. Turn left and follow this until it reaches the "B5026" road. Go left and then cross the road with care as the corners obscure the sight of oncoming vehicles.

4. At the corner turn right to cross a stile by a barred gate and keep ahead alongside a hedge. Mid way along cross a stile into an adjacent field and now follow the hedge on the left for a short level stretch before heading down the field towards the sheltered waters of Copmere. Join the thick boundary hedge of the mere, a disappointment as it is only possible to catch glimpses of the rippling waters through the thick growth. Go left and follow the well-worn path around the mere to a ladder stile which exits onto a lane. Make a right turn for The Star at Copmere before the last leg back to Eccleshall.

5. Retrace your steps along the road, passing by the ladder stile, towards the hamlet of Pershall. Pershall pool can be glimpsed on the left. Opposite Pershall Lodge, look for a stile leading into a field. Within a few paces cross another stile beneath a tree. Then, proceed slightly left across the field to a gate by a house and to the road.

6. Turn next right and just beyond a farm known as The Hough, as the lane begins to curve right, go through a gate. Head slightly right across the field to cross a little stile and then the path curves left, up to an awkward stile to climb by a gate. Once on the road go almost immediately left through another gate. Head slightly left up the field to a small gate and then continue straight on to go through another gate in the next boundary, across an area known as The Leys. Proceed in a similar direction and then follow the hedge which soon dips and curves. Look for a stile here on the left. Cross it and below stands Eccleshall, the church a landmark for miles around. The gentle descent through this last pasture to a kissing gate between houses somehow seems an appropriate end to the walk. The path squeezes between gardens to Church Street and back to High Street.

# 5. FAIROAK

**Route:** Fair Oak – Bishop's Wood – Croxton – Rookery Cottages – Fair Oak

**Distance:** 5 miles

**Map:** O.S. Pathfinder 829 Market Drayton

**Start:** The Freemasons Arms (Grid Reference: SJ 766326)

**Access:** Unfortunately, there is a very sparse bus service. Check with Staffordshire Bus on (0785) 223344.

*By Car* – Fairoak is half a mile off the B5026 between Loggerheads and Eccleshall turning either at Wetwood farm or near Broughton church. There is limited car parking beyond the crossroads in the hamlet.

## The Freemasons Arms, Fair Oak (0630) 82284

This old public house has survived in one of the quietest backwaters of the county. The name stems from a Masonic gathering in earlier times and an old inn sign reflects this in the large lounge bar. Do not worry – there is no secret code or special handshake required these days to secure a drink or meal here!

There is one long bar in the lounge and a smaller bar serving a back room with a snooker table. The pub usually serves the Theakston's range of beers including the treacly Old Peculier which can have the effect of making the ramble seem surreal so if sampling this brew try it in halves. Families are welcome and bar meals are available at most times. The Freemasons is open from 7pm in the evening on Mondays to Fridays (ie not lunchtimes) but is open all day on Saturdays. Usual Sunday hours are observed.

*The Freemason's Arms*

## Fair Oak

The small hamlet borders the expansive Bishop's Wood where wood burning and glass making were strong local industries. On the ramble, there is a glass furnace which has been excavated and partially restored. In the 17th century the industry moved south to what is now known as The Black Country.

# The Walk

(1) At the crossroads, make your way left down a bridleway festooned in summer with vetch, rosebay, blackberry and rose-hip. To the right stands a wood covered tumulus. The track curves right to pass Moss Farm and then opens into a field. There is a track leading off to the right but keep ahead by a hedge.

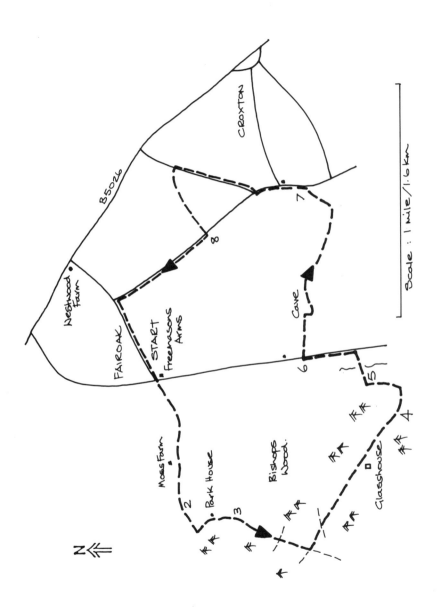

Scale : 1 mile / 1.6 km

*Leaving Bishop's Wood*

(2) You will catch a glimpse of Park House from here. The path leads towards the wood but curves back left towards the house. Proceed through the main barred gate and then keep ahead between the garage and garden, the house now being to your left. Cross a stile by the next barred gate and climb up between gorse and scrub bushes to Bishop's Wood by way of the bridle gate.

(3) This is a large plantation with many forest tracks, so be vigilant. Go straight on and ahead at the junction. The track begins to descend and you catch a glimpse of hills through the trees. You will also see a junction ahead but turn left beforehand onto a lesser path. Cross the main forestry track and proceed ahead. At the next junction keep ahead but at this point, on your right, is the restored glasshouse. The track leads towards a gateway and open field.

(4) The right of way proceeds through the gate and follows the field's edge on the left around to the corner where a stile allows the walker to

cut left back on to a forest path. Local walkers, however, tend to simply follow the well-worn path to the left of the gateway which curves left along the perimeter of the wood.

(5) You will see houses across a field on the Fair Oak road. Look for a stile here on the right which leads into a wet meadow. The path leads slightly left to a bridge over the infant River Sow. Continue in a similar direction towards a bungalow and cross a stile onto the road. Turn left and walk towards Fair Oak. This is a possible cut-off point for those seeking a shorter ramble.

(6) As you approach a farm go through a barred gate opposite a large oak. Keep to the right of the wire fencing and go to the top right gateway. It is feasible to cross this,despite the strand of barbed wire. To the left is an area which was once orcharded and follow the field edge ahead to a scar and cave. It is dangerous, so keep away from the outcrop as you follow the path. It curves right up to a stile in the top of the field corner. Cross this and keep company with the hedge on your right to cross another stile. This leads into a large open field where you proceed ahead to the brow and then onwards to a stile. Cross this and go right along the green lane. At the junction go left and walk up an impressive sandstone cutting. In the distance the old windmill at Croxton can be seen.

(7) At the road junction turn left and soon pass a farm. At the next corner, as the road bends left, keep ahead along a bridleway which descends gradually to pass a small farm and then look for the next turn left before entering Croxton itself. This track leads by houses and gardens. Before an entrance to a cottage, bear left along a narrower hedged grassy path. This very shortly arrives at a barred gate. Go through it and turn left up the field hedge, by an electricity pylon and then through another gate. Keep ahead in the next field to a third gate exiting onto a road.

(8) Go right, following the road by Rookery Cottages to a junction. Turn left here to descend to Fair Oak.

# 6. STONE

**Route:** Stone – Trent & Mersey Canal – Meaford Locks – Oulton – Cotwalton – Stone

**Distance:** 6 miles

**Map:** O.S. Pathfinder 830 Stone (Staffordshire)

**Start:** The Star, Stone (Grid Reference: SJ 903337)

**Access:** Stone is served by train and bus from The Potteries and Stafford. Train enquiries (0782) 411411 or 'phone Staffordshire Busline on (0785) 223344

*By Car* – Travel on the A34 to Stone, turning left at Walton roundabout for Stone. There is limited parking near Walton Bridge.

## The Star, Stone (0785) 813096

The Star Inn stands by the Trent and Mersey canal and many sit outside to watch the boats go by in Summer. The original building, however, pre dates the canal by many a century. It is thought to have medieval origins and was definitely registered as an ale-house in the 16th century.

When this section of the canal was completed in the early 1770s the good townspeople of Stone fired a canon at the lock-side by The Star. Unfortunately, their aim was a little askew and a large hole appeared in the lock gates and some bridge masonry crumbled too. Needless to say, the worthy gathering shrugged their shoulders and repaired to The Star to discuss the unfortunate incident.

A visitor might assume that the beverages dispensed here have immediate effect, for the rooms appear to be at different levels. Do not worry as this is reality! The number of small rooms is one of the appealing aspects of the pub which is open all day during Summer (April to October) and from 11am until 3pm in the Winter on Mondays to Saturday lunchtimes. Evening opening is from 5.30 pm. Usual Sunday hours prevail. Food is available until 3pm and from 6 to 9pm daily. Banks's Mild and Bitter and Marstons Pedigree are served at this enterprising hostelry.

*The Star*

## Stone

The small town of Stone with its bustling High Street has grown up around the canal and railway, the station being a superb piece of architecture dating from 1848. Stone has many pubs and was once the home of Joules Brewery. Some of this complex survives, although it is no longer used for brewing.

# The Walk

(1) Pass by The Star public house along the towpath in the direction of Stoke-on-Trent. The canal passes the much loved Joules brewery and under the road, the railway and into open countryside. It then approaches Meaford locks. Come off at Bridge Number 97.

(2) Turn right to walk along the lane but look for a path on the left by the drive for Meaford Old Hall farm. The path curves right to pass beneath the railway across a bridge by a ford. The path is corralled as it leads to a track with the farm to the left. Follow this to a bridge over a stream. Cross a stile and then keep company with a hedge on the right to exit onto a narrow road.

(3) Go left and almost immediately turn right to walk up to a crossroads. Cross over and then turn left at next junction into Kibblestone Road. Pass the entrance to Oulton Grange on the left and then Oulton Abbey, an old convent on the right which is now a residential home. Walk by the Brushmakers Arms, an interesting village local, and turn right into Church Lane. Turn left opposite the Post Office and, after modern houses, leave the village of Oulton. The road narrows into a cutting and descends to the main A520 road.

(4) Turn right along the main road towards Ivy Mill. Pass Grove House and cross over to walk up a metalled lane by it. Go left and then first right up the lane signposted to Cotwalton, a quiet backwater lying half way between Stone and Hilderstone. At the junction keep ahead to soon pass the entrance of Home Farm and before a bungalow cross a stile on the right. The path is signposted.

(5) Head diagonally across the field with the chimneys of Meaford power station in the distance. Cross a double stile and then head slightly left over the next field to a sleeper bridge and stile. Cross both and head in a similar direction to cross another double stile and sleeper bridge, again heading in the same direction. Cross a stile by a gate and walk slightly left through a long field. Dip down to the indent to cross a stile and footbridge.

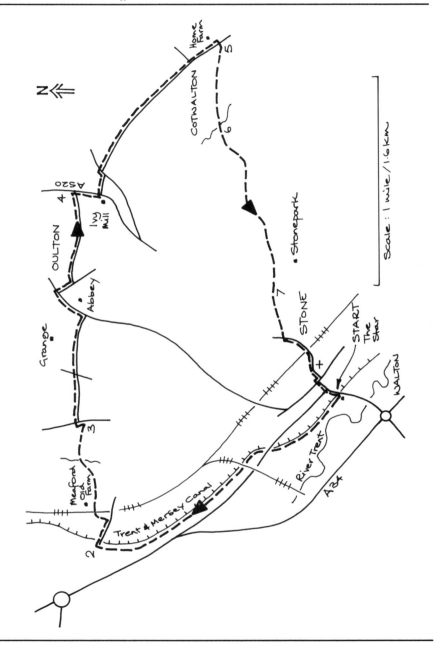

(6) The path winds up the other side of the valley to step up to a stile and into fields again. Pass to the right of an electricity pylon and follow wire fencing up to a stile situated to the left of a gate. Cross the stile and turn right along the brow of the hill, with exceptional views over the county. Go through a gateway and follow the track as it curves left up to a gate. Cross the stile and climb the track by the small wood with Stonepark farm to the left. At the junction keep right.

(7) The track descends to Redhill Road on the outskirts of Stone where an old mill is seen to the right and a little further along pass The Swan public house. Cross the railway tracks and on the left is a church. At the main road turn right and next left. Keep ahead to cross the Trent and Mersey Canal and return to The Star pub.

*The Trent and Mersey canal, near Stone*

# 7. SWYNNERTON

**Route:** Swynnerton – Cotes – Cranberry – Swynnerton

**Distance:** 4 miles

**Map:** O.S. Pathfinder 830 Stone (Staffordhire)

**Start:** The Fitzherbert Arms, Swynnerton (Grid Reference: SJ 853356)

**Access:** Swynnerton has a limited bus service on Mondays to Saturdays. Contact Staffordshire Bus for details on (0785) 223344.

*By Car* – Travel on the A519 towards Eccleshall turning left at the juction with the A51 then next right for Swynnerton.

## The Fitzherbert Arms (0781) 35542

The Fitzherbert Arms has served the villages of the area well over the decades, a traditional house with two rooms offering a fine pint of Draught Bass. The pub also offers bar snacks and a restaurant. Bar food is available at lunch until 1.45pm and in the evenings until 9.45pm every day. The Fitzherbert Arms is open from 11.00am until 3pm Mondays to Saturdays and from 7pm at night. Usual Sunday hours are observed. Families are welcome and there are seats outside when the weather is fine.

## Swynnerton

Swynnerton is very much an estate village surrounded mainly by parkland belonging to Swynnerton Hall, a mansion built in classical style during the early part of the 18th century. Unusually, there are two large churches in the village, a parish church dating from Norman times and a Roman Catholic church from the Victorian period. The latter was built by the Fitzherbert family who have resided in the hall since the mid-16th century, the previous residents being the Swynnertons. The present Lord Stafford resides in the Hall which is not open to the public.

*Swynnerton village*

# The Walk

(1) From the Fitzherbert Arms turn right and walk along the main street as it bends right. Turn right by houses with the village cricket ground on the left. Look for a stile on the left beyond the gateway.

(2) Cross the stile and proceed ahead, keeping to the right of the pitch then to the left of a group of trees. Continue across the field to a stile situated to the right of a pool. Walk through a small wood turning right to exit over a stile. Go straight on, keeping company with the fence. Cross two stiles to reach a road in Cotes.

(3) Turn right and at the corner keep ahead along a bridleway, with hedgerows rich in plant life. The way narrows and passes to the rear of an industrial estate. At the end of the perimeter fence go left over a stile and walk along the field's edge to the main road. Cross with care.

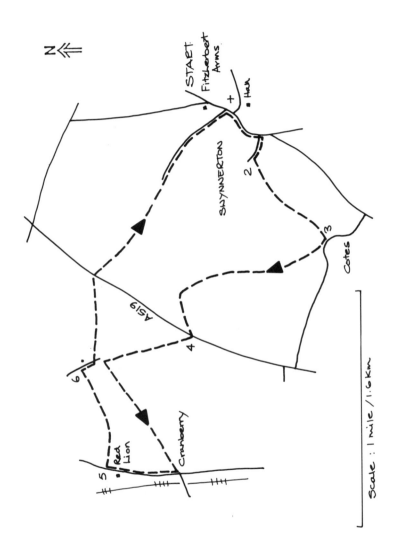

(4) Go through the wooden barred gate and follow the tractor tracks ahead. Go through another gate before coming to a junction. Turn left and follow this bridle route to houses in the hamlet of Cranberry. Turn right at the crossroads. Fast trains speed by this otherwise sleepy place. Pass the village stores and Red Lion public house.

(5) Just beyond, look for a stile on the right between hedges. The path comes to a stile which leads to a field. Turn right to walk up the field keeping company with a hedge on the right. Cross a large stile beneath a tree and head slightly left in the next field along the bank. Cross the stile and continue ahead with the hedge to your right. Cross another stile to join a track.

(6) Turn right and pass a solitary rustic cottage. Turn next left (as signposted) to follow the field's edge to the main road. Cross over and proceed along a well-worn path up the field. Continue to a gap on the left allowing the track to switch to the other side of the hedge. Go straight on to the next boundary then turn right. Join a track which becomes a metalled road, known as Early Lane. At the main road turn left for The Fitzherbert Arms.

*The Fitzherbert Arms*

# 8. ASHLEY

**Route:** Robin Hood – Ashley – Ashley Church – Middle Coppice – Podmore – Podmore Pool – Charnes Road – Jugbank – Robin Hood

**Distance:** 5 miles

**Map:** O.S. Pathfinder 829 Market Drayton

**Start:** The Robin Hood, Ashley (Grid Reference: 754357) or some might wish to start at Ashley Church (Grid Reference: 763364) where there is a little more on-street parking available.

**Access:** There is a daily bus to Ashley except Sundays. Contact Staffordshire Busline for details.

*By Car* – Travel on the A53 from Newcastle-Under-Lyme towards Loggerheads where you turn either first or second left to Ashley after crossing the A51 road.

## The Robin Hood (0630) 872237

The Robin Hood is tucked away on a back road off the Loggerheads to Eccleshall Road at Jugbank. It is well known in the area for its restaurant but also has an open lounge where walkers are made most welcome. The Robin Hood offers Burtonwood Bitter and Thomas Forshaws on draught and bar meals are available at lunch and during the evenings. Opening times are noon until 2.30pm (3pm on Saturdays) at lunchtimes except Monday when the pub is closed. Evening opening is at 6pm. Usual Sunday hours. Please note that the car park is for patrons only and those seeking parking might wish to park near to the church instead.

## Ashley

Ashley is a sprawling village found along lanes off the main A53 road to Market Drayton, lanes which lead to the nucleus of the village, the parish church. This fascinating little place of worship houses a very large alabaster tomb from the early 17th century, and several splendid

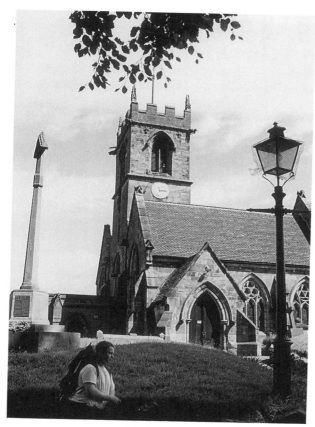

*Ashley Church*

Victorian monuments belonging to landowning Kinnersley and Meynell families. All these families were influential in the village but none resided here, the nearest location being Gerrards Bromley which can be seen on the return section of the walk from Podmore pool.

Ashley was a popular ride out from The Potteries in the earlier decades of this century as local belief was that the wooded slopes and fresh air of Ashley make for a beneficial break from the urban grime. People would take tea at The Meynell Arms before returning of an afternoon. In many respects, the village has not altered much since, and the air does feel good here. Walk a few fields and see if you agree.

# The Walk

(1) Turn left from the entrance to the Robin Hood public house in the direction of Ashley, the road bending right and left. Ignore turnings to the left, pass The Croft and at the next corner go right along a little pathway which brings you to a drive and road. Turn right to pass a shop and church in Ashley.

(2) Opposite the Meynell Arms, go right down a track by an old cottage. Cross the stile by a gate and follow the track to cross stiles by barred gates into a field. Keep ahead through the next field to cross another stile by a gate. Go straight on but keep to the left of an electricity pole and oak tree. Meet a hedge and ditch. Look for the double stile and bridge towards the corner.

(3) Once over go right to the corner, then turn left to walk for 50 paces to a stile on the right(ie beyond the gate). Cross the stile and footbridge then bear slightly left towards the wood. Go right at the wood's edge up to a stile. Cross here and head slightly right in the pasture, passing a pool to a stile by a gate. Once over keep ahead to cross another stile with Podmore farm on the left. Continue forward to cross a stile and down steps to a road.

(4) Turn right along the lane as it descends to a small bridge over the brook. Go over the stile on the right. Head slightly left up the bank away from Podmore pool. Cross a stile in a wire fence to the right of a mound. Walk straight on through a large field often in cereal crop and there are views to the left to Gerrards Bromley mentioned earlier. Local legend has it that the estate was lost in gambling by the last Lord Gerrard to a Meynell. Cross two stiles guarding a gully. Keep ahead to go through a gateway with large poles on either side.

(5) Go straight on to cross a stile by a gate. In the next field head slightly right in the direction of an electricity pole mid field passing to the right of a pool. Cross a double stile and head towards the houses of Ashley. Proceed through the rough pasture to join a field corner. Walk past the water trough with the hedge on the right. Cross the stile on the right. Head slightly left across the field to a stile leading into a road.

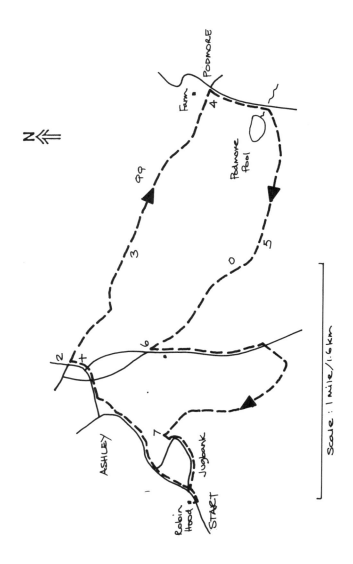

(6) Turn left to follow the road as it descends by Bridgebank Cottage. The road rises and your way is up a bank to cross a boundary fence. Head slightly left, crossing the field towards a gate but at the opposite hedge go right, following the boundary to a gateway which enters a pasture. Proceed down the bank to pass a line of oaks to a wider dry valley. There is a barn ahead. The path dips down to a stream bed and beneath an embankment go right here with the stream bed to your right. The path curves left beneath the farm into a green lane. Go through a kissing gate and keep ahead by a secluded cottage on the right.

(7) As the track bears slightly right go left over a ladder stile and through a kissing gate. Head slightly left up the bank to cross a stile into a lane. Go left. The lane curves around to the right and the joins the outward route at a junction. Turn left for the Robin Hood at Jug Bank.

*The Robin Hood*

# 9. CHURCH LEIGH

**Route:** Church Leigh – Park Hall – Brook Lane – Upper Leigh – Church Leigh church – Bents Farm – Withington – Church Leigh

**Distance:** 3.5 miles

**Map:** O.S. Pathfinder 831 Uttoxeter

**Start:** The Star, Church Leigh (Grid Reference: 027358)

**Access:** There is no real access by bus to Church Leigh.

*By Car* – Church Leigh is not an easy place to find. It is best approached by turning right off the old A50 road at Tean onto a lane which runs under the A40 then turn left for about 2 – 3 miles through to Church Leigh. There is limited on-street parking in the village near The Star Inn and church.

---

## The Star (0889) 502453

The Star is an attractive pub standing between the church and village stores. It serves Tetley Bitter and Burton Ale, and a guest beer on a rotation basis from a small central bar which caters for three separate areas. Bar snacks are available throughout the week and traditional Sunday lunch is served in this homely hostelry. Families are welcome but there is no garden at The Star. Opening times are at 7pm each evening, i.e. there are no lunchtime sessions except Saturday when The Star opens from noon until 3pm. Usual Sunday hours. Take a look at the picture of the snow drifts by the front door on the way out. Is this a feature of the past?

## The Farmers Arms, Withington (0889) 502274

The Farmers Arms is in the hamlet of Withington, a pub which attracts local people from nearby villages and farmsteads. There's a cosy large bar, often with an open fire in winter as well as a separate restaurant area. The walls exhibit traditional brass ornaments and the occasional musical instrument. Altogether, this is a friendly country pub. The Farmers serves Marstons Pedigree and Draught Bass and sells food until 9.30pm on weekday evenings and at Sunday lunchtime until 1.30pm. Opening times are 7pm each evening and Sunday lunch from noon until 3 pm. Families are welcome and there are seats outside.

*The Farmers Arms*

# Church Leigh

The most striking feature of this village is the commanding tower of the church, built in the 1840s by the Bagot family on a site occupied by places of worship since Saxon times. This is one of the many hamlets that grew up in the lush Blythe valley, communities which have retained their agricultural base to this day. The walk also passes through Upper Leigh and near to Lower Leigh – clusters of houses on intertwining lanes in this unknown part of the county.

*The impressive Manor at Lower Leigh*

# The Walk

(1) From the Star turn left and just before the post office, turn left again. Turn right up Lime Close between bungalows to a stile which exits into a large field. Keep ahead through the field to a point parallel with a gate on the right and head slightly left. The landmark is a point to the left of a large barn belonging to Park Hall, once the home of landowners Lord and Lady Aston whose tombs are in the church, with those of their thirteen offspring. The path leaves the field through a large gate.

(2) Turn left along the road, past a bungalow on the right and then by the drive on the right to Brookfield Head Farm. Turn next left down a narrow lane, known appropriately as Brook Lane, a minor thoroughfare festooned with fresh red campion, burr and other roadside plants. This descends to a brook and then climbs up to a junction by Yew Tree Farm in Upper Leigh. Turn left and the road bends right shortly by a rear entrance to Manor House. Go through the kissing gate on the left and walk to another. Once through keep ahead along the drive away from the house. The road dips to a little bridge and then climbs to an entrance onto the Church Leigh road.

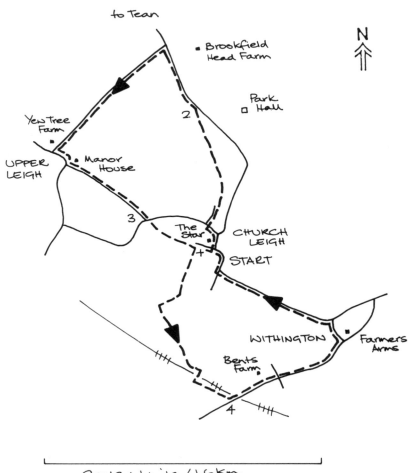

Scale : 1 mile / 1.6 Km

(3) Cross over and walk through a pasture behind houses. Go through a kissing a gate into a playing field and continue ahead through another kissing gate into the churchyard. Pass to the right of the church and by the Victorian lamp turn right along a path between gravestones to a kissing gate which leads to a large gently-sloping pasture. Keep company with the hedge to the left and make your way through a gateway. Follow the hedge on the left again ahead at first then left until it reaches a barred gate. Go through it and walk alongside the Derby to Stoke railway line to a green lane. Do not go left, however. Instead turn right to cross the tracks with extreme caution. Once over go immediately left through a gap in a hedge. Walk through the field to a road.

(4) Turn left to pass Bents Farm and keep ahead at the crossroads. This leads to Withington where the Farmers Arms is at the first junction. Turn left here and at the next junction left again along the road to Church Leigh. Readers might like to know that the authors have requested that a path across fields before Crossways to Church Leigh be cleared to provide an off-road route. Hopefully, this will be incorporated in future editions but at the time of writing the path suffered far too many obstructions to recommend with confidence.

*The Star, Church Leigh*

# 10. MODDERSHALL

**Route:** Moddershall – Idlerocks – Stallington Heath – Mossgate – Spot Gate Inn – Moddershall

**Distance:** 5 miles

**Map:** O.S. Pathfinder Stone 830 (Staffs)

**Start:** The Boar, Moddershall (Grid Reference: 927367)

**Access:** Moddershall is served by a regular daily bus service from Hanley. Contact PMT on (0782) 747000 for details.

*By Car* – Moddershall can be approached from the A520 Stone to Meir Heath road or from the B5066 to Hilderstone. There is limited on-street parking near to The Boar or village hall.

## The Boar (0782) 372493

The Boar stands within the shade of a wooded bank by an old mill pond, a setting which inspires the rambler at any time of the year. The pub has a welcoming bar where darts and other games are played and an impressive lounge where a large mirror rests over a traditional fireplace. There are many legends about the pub including one about a ghost which returns occasionally. The ghost is that of a weary soldier said to have hung himself in an outbuilding rather than return to the gruesome front in World War II.

The Boar is open from noon until 3pm on Mondays to Saturdays and from 7pm in the evening. During the summer these hours are extended to all day. Usual Sunday hours prevail. Food is available at all sessions and families are welcome. There is an extensive play area outside and children love the menagerie of ducks, geese and other fowl who waddle in and out of the water, a great source of amusement to the onlooker.

*The Boar, Moddershall*

## The Spot Gate (0889) 505277

The Spot Gate is on the HIlderstone Road. For many years it has caught the eye of many a passer-by for, behind the main pub, are two 1929 Pullman railway coaches, restored as a restaurant. The First coach is named Ursula and the Second class coach "Car 75"! A detailed history of the coaches is told on two plaques inside. The one carriage is allegedly haunted and while sightings have come from waiting staff over the years no one is quite sure why the ghostly happenings occur.

The spacious pub offers Ansells Traditional Bitter and Ind Coope Burton Ale, also Draught Bass for the thirsty rambler. Those with families will find the patio and children's adventure play area of an exceptionally high standard and at certain times there is a "pop shop" open! Food (Bar snacks, bistro and restaurant) is served at lunch until 2pm and in the evening until 9.30pm. Pub opening times are from noon until 3pm and from 7pm in the evening on Mondays to Fridays and all day on Saturdays. Usual Sunday hours. This is a very accommodating hostelry.

## Moddershall

Moddershall, lying amid gently rising hills north of Stone is a village which has fallen back into agricultural ways having witnessed a hint of industrialisation in earlier times. What looks to be the tiniest of brooks supplied the power to drive several mills in the neighbourhood. These were built originally to process corn but then adapted to grind flint for the emergent pottery manufacturing world a few miles away. One such mill, Mosty Lee at Lower Moddershall, is the subject of restoration, another Ivy Mill is a listed building.

# The Walk

(1) Start from the Boar Inn. With your back to the pub entrance, bear left to walk towards the village for a short distance before turning first left up a narrow road signposted to Hilltop. The road soon leads to a track, climbing across the little valley and up a bank past houses. It continues ahead at first but then curves right and becomes a woodland path

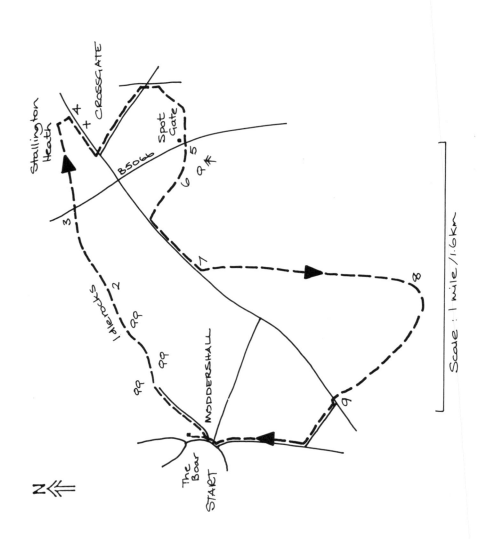

climbing up a narrow valley, with fencing to the right at first. The wooded slopes and outcrops to the left are known as Idlerocks and a Victorian house of the same name lies beyond but cannot be seen from here.

(2) The well-worn path eventually exits the wood at a stile by a holly tree. Keep ahead up the field with a hedge to your left, along a section which can get muddy. The path follows an old trackway up to another stile. Cross it and walk through rough pasture bearing very slightly right up the bank to the brow of the field where a track can be seen on the right. Follow this ahead as it curves gently right to the main B5066 road.

(3) Cross the road and a stile into a wood at Stallington Heath. Keep ahead along the path which runs parallel to a track, with markers on several tree stumps. This soon leads to another stile. Cross it and turn left in a clearing. The path soon joins woodland again (assuming that the wood has not been cleared since the walk was researched). The path continues ahead and comes to a fence where it bears slightly left at first and then right with the fence to your right. It joins a track. Turn right here to the road.

(4) Go right to pass a chapel dating from 1860 on the left. At the next road junction bear left along Moss Lane. This reaches another junction where you turn right into Balaams Lane. Opposite the row of houses, go right along a track between holly hedges. The track leads to a house but your way is to the right of the garden along a hedged green path which leads to a stile. Cross this and go to the right to wander down a sunken green lane between gorse and a hedge towards a white building, The Spot Gate public house. Cross the stile to the right at the rear of the pullman carriages, a stile which should be treated with care as there are bits of barbed wire tangled around it. Go to the front car park.

(5) Cross the road opposite the pub and walk along a track which curves to the left of a gate and into a wood and then ahead. This comes to a barred gate which you go through. Your way is ahead through a little wicket gate (although in recent years there has been tipping here and some ramblers cut left and right to walk along the field's edge, through a gap and right over a bridge to re join the true line). Once through the wicket gate, however, the path runs ahead along the side of a bank through undergrowth. Go through old gateposts and continue ahead

through semi jungle conditions between scrub and rhododendrons. In Spring there is a sea of bluebells here which are a joy to see.

(6) Pass by a little footbridge on the left and follow the path alongside the drainage ditch out of the wood and into a field. Walk up to the gate and turn left on the road. Walk by a house on the left and as the road begins to curve left then right by a wood look for a stile. The best landmark to look for is a large aerial seen to the left across a field, and served by a track on the left. Do not go down here.

(7) Instead look for two gates just to the right of this track and there is a stile here which leads into a wide green lane, obviously a road of importance in the past. Follow this as it widens and descends in the direction of Stone. The view is panoramic across West Staffordshire, to The Wrekin and Shropshire high hills beyond. A wood is to the right and at this point there is a cross path. However, your way is down to the bottom fence where a stile is crossed to enter a large field. Head slightly left here and go through a kissing gate to enter a track.

(8) This becomes a green track between fences running alongside a drainage ditch. Go through a wicket gate and look for a stile on the right beyond the sheltered pool. Head slightly right to a field corner and then proceed ahead to cross a stile in a hedge. Walk straight on to go over a stile by a gate. Bear slightly left in the next field to dip down to another stile which is crossed. Go ahead to a penultimate stile before climbing the bank to exit by way of the last stile which is found to the right of a gate.

(9) Cross the road and follow the quiet lane down the hillside into Moddershall. Turn right to walk back into the village passing by one of the old established nurseries in this area.

# 11. BARLASTON

**Route:** Barlaston Railway Station – Wedgwood – Barlaston Green – Trent and Mersey Canal – Barlaston Railway Station

**Distance:** 3.5 miles

**Map:** O.S. Pathfinder Map 830 (Stone)

**Start:** Barlaston Railway station (Grid reference: SJ 887384)

**Access:** There is a train service from Stoke-on-Trent, Stone and Stafford which runs daily except Sundays. There is also a regular PMT bus from Hanley to Barlaston. Contact PMT on (0782) 747000 for details.

*By Car* – Travel on the A34 south of Newcastle-Under-Lyme to Tittersor where a left turn is made for Barlaston. There is car parking at Barlaston Green where the walk can be started if not arriving by train.

## The Duke of York, Barlaston (0782) 372580

The Duke of York is an attractive looking village local with its white walls and pub sign beckoning the walker inside. The front bar is cosier than the larger lounge to the rear but on either side hand-pulled draught Bass is available, a well kept pint much loved by the regular clientele. Connoisseurs of bottled ales might like to try Worthington White Shield, a very traditional bottled real ale which has been re packaged for the 1990s evidently to make the drink more appealing, as if it needed any extra appeal. The pub is open from 11am until 3pm on Mondays to Thursdays, extending to 4pm on Fridays and 4.30pm on Saturdays. Evening opening at 6pm. Usual Sunday hours. Bar meals are available on Monday to Saturday lunchtimes only and families are welcome at lunchtimes but not evening sessions.

## Barlaston

Barlaston is perhaps best known as the home of Wedgwood, the world-renowned ceramics manufacturer who moved out of town in the

1930s to establish a factory in the countryside. The Museum and Visitor Centre includes an extensive collection of pottery dating from the time of the founding father, Josiah Wedgwood to modern designs. While tours of the factory are not available, the visitor centre includes demonstrations of the traditional skills such as throwing pots, etc.

The walk passes by the three storeys of Barlaston Hall. This hall was built in the 1750s for Thomas Mills, a wealthy lawyer. When Wedgwood bought the estate they gained ownership of the hall which was in a poor state of repair. The hall has since changed ownership through the decades and it is said that it was bought for £1 on the condition that it was restored. Thankfully, that is exactly what has happened in recent years.

*Barlaston Hall*

Barlaston village has developed around the picturesque green, and on the south side of the railway station and canal, making it a rather sprawling settlement. The old school now houses a library.

*The Duke of York, featured on this walk*

# The Walk

(1) From Barlaston station turn right to pass by Barlaston News, then over the canal bridge to a road, known as canal-side, leading right by The Plume and Feathers, another popular pub in Barlaston which serves Bass beers. Join the towpath and turn left to walk beside the Trent and Mersey Canal. The path soon leaves the village and there is a good view of the statue of the Duke of Sutherland on Tittensor Hill. It is less than a mile to Wedgwood, where you exit at Bridge 104.

(2) Go right over the bridge and then bear right over a stile by a gate within a few metres. Nearby is the Wedgwood factory. The well-worn track leads across the field to the railway tracks to the right of Wedgwood railway station. Cross with extreme caution for the London trains thunder through at considerable speed.

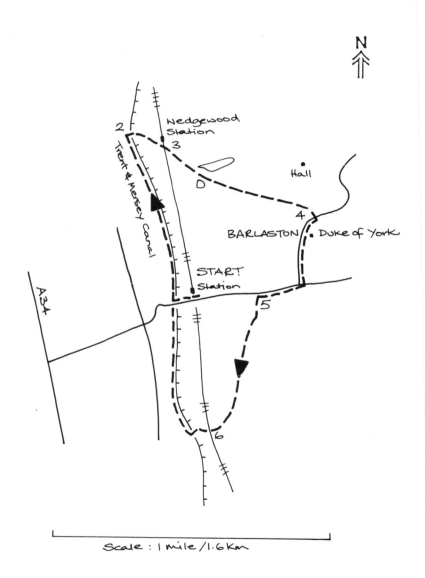

Scale : 1 mile / 1.6 Km

(3) The path now heads slightly right across the next field to cross a stile. Then go slightly left to proceed through a gate and cross the head of a pool, used by fishermen from Wedgwood. You can see Barlaston Hall from here and the path offers a clear view of the hall as you progress across the fields. Go through the kissing gate and keep ahead in a similar direction to cross a stile mid field and another at the next boundary. The well-worn path leads to a road here.

(4) Turn right and soon pass the Duke of York public house to Barlaston Green where a restored cross stands. To the right is Barlaston old school, now a library. Bear right to walk down Station Road but cross over by the modern church to cross a stile by a gate.

(5) Follow a track along the left side of the field and go through a gateway into the next field. Turn right and keep company with the hedge to the right. The path leads into the corner where a little ladder stile is climbed. Walk through a pocket of woodland to cross an old stile. In the next field go left keeping the hedge to your left. Towards the railway line look for a stile on the left under a tree which leads to a track.

(6) Turn right to walk under the railway, then follow the track around to the right then left to the canal bridge. Cross the bridge and walk down to the towpath on the left. Bear left to walk under the bridge and along the last section to The Plume and Feathers. Retrace your steps to Barlaston station.

# 12. HOLLINGTON

**Route:** Hollington – The Raddle Inn – Croxden – Hollington

**Distance:** 2.5 miles

**Map:** O.S. Pathfinder 831 Uttoxeter

**Start:** The Village Stores, Hollington (Grid Reference: 055391)

**Access:** Hollington has a very limited bus service from Hanley and Uttoxeter.

*By Car* – follow the A50 to Tean, turning left onto the Hollington Road. The Stores stands by the junction for Greatgate. There is limited on-street parking near to the junction by the village hall and stores.

## The Star Inn (0889) 26250

The Star is a traditional red sandstone built pub standing alongside the Hollington Road in the middle of the village which is well frequented by locals but also caters for visitors coming to the area. The homely bar offers three cask conditioned ales from Marstons – Border Exhibition, Burton Bitter and Pedigree, and Theakstons Bitter. Food is served at lunchtimes at the weekend up until 1.30pm and every evening until 9.30pm.

The Star Inn welcomes families and has a patio area outside when the weather is kind. It is not open at lunchtimes except weekends when the times are noon until 3 pm. Evening opening is 7 pm. An ideal spot to finish your ramble.

## The Raddle Inn (O889) 26278

The Raddle is situated part way along the ramble and is a good place to sit out on a summers day as the view across to Croxden Abbey is marvellous. The unusual name stems from the local quarrying activity. The Landlord has checked the deeds and the inn was originally called

The Masons Arms. There are compass and square signs above both fireplaces suggesting the connection with Freemasons in earlier times. Nevertheless, older people recollect that the pub was always known as The Raddle, a name referring to the red pigment brought in on the boots of the stonemasons. The name was officially changed about ten years ago in recognition of this tradition.

The Raddle offers draught Bass, Pedigree, Boddingtons Bitter, Whitbread Castle Eden and Theakstons Old Peculier. It also serves food at lunch until 2pm and during the evening until 10 pm. Opening times are noon until 3pm and from 7pm in the evening. Usual Sunday opening. One couldn't find a more pleasant spot for a pub.

*The Raddle Inn*

## Hollington

The high moorland village of Hollington, on the old Roman road from Tean to Rocester is a part of the county that few walkers visit. The parish is threaded by a network of beautiful local paths but far too many of these are obstructed or in poor condition. Hollington is well endowed with stone built dwellings, the distinctive red stone having been hewn from local quarries. The little Victorian church standing on a bluff at the top end of the village is well cared for by this isolated community.

*Croxden Abbey*

## Croxden

The majestic ruins of Croxden Abbey are the highlight of this ramble. The Cistercian ruins, dating from the 12th century, are quite extensive, yet this monument is little known even in the county. The religious collective would have worked the land throughout the ages until dissolution and the story of life here is told on interpretation boards throughout the buildings which are open at any reasonable hour.

# The Walk

(1) Start from a road junction at Hollington (near the stores and village hall) on the left well before the Star public house, signposted to Greatgate. Walk down the metalled road beneath the wooded scars of earlier quarries to The Raddle Inn.

*The Star, at Hollington*

(2) Just opposite the pub turn right down a tractor track. As the track corners, bear slightly right again along a green track but within a hundred paces or so turn right by gorse bushes down a bank. The path dips to a stone gap-stile which is virtually hidden below. The is the path not clear on the ground, but the stile is the key marker. Once through head slightly left near to the old boundary stone marked with the initials CH/CR part-way down the field. Cross a tractor track and go through a stile by a water trough.

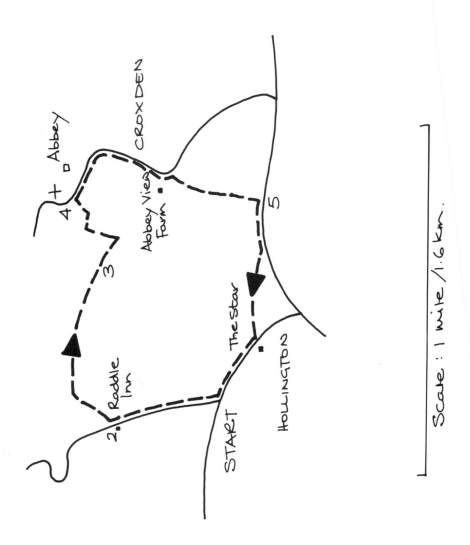

Scale : 1 mile / 1.6 km.

(3) Proceed ahead with a fence on the left to a gap-stile in the corner. Go through it and continue ahead to the next field corner, catching glimpses of Croxden abbey behind the farm. Bear left now to cross wet ground by the Croxden brook to a gap-stile by a gate. Follow the track as it bears right to pass the rear of Abbey farm buildings. It then curves left up to a metalled road in the hamlet of Croxden. Turn left to see Croxden church and right for the Abbey, taking care to enter the latter by way of the main entrance and not the drive on the right to a private residence.

(4) From the entrance to the abbey turn right and follow the lane around to the right. This comes to a corner by Abbey View Farm. Just beyond the corner is a stile on the right. Go over it and walk up the field to a stone gap-stile. Once through head slightly right up the bank to a hollow and pass over a stile. There is a pool to the left. Cross the field to the right of a gate and cross a stile onto the road, then turn right.

(5) At the corner dip down to the small lay-by and cross a stile on the right by a gate into the field. Head left up the field alongside a hedge, then cut across towards a farmhouse where a stile is crossed and then another exits onto the road. Go right to pass the Star public house and return to the starting point.

# 13. MADELEY

**Route:** Madeley church – Furnace Lane – Mill Cottages – Near Wrinehill Mill – Lowermill House – Madeley church

**Distance:** 4 miles

**Map:** O.S. Pathfinder 808 Audlem

**Start:** Madeley Church (Grid Reference: 773444)

**Access:** There is a regular daily bus to Madeley. Contact Staffordshire Bus on (0785) 223344 for details. The bus pulls up between the church and public car park at the start of the walk.

*By Car* – travel on the A525 from Newcastle-under-Lyme. The car park is behind Madeley Church.

## The Offley Arms (0782) 750242

This tall and large Victorian public house has in recent years been renovated, and there are several areas served from one central bar. Hand-pulled Whitbread Flowers, Allied Tetley and Marstons Pedigree are on offer and food is served. Families are welcome and there is an outdoor drinking area. The Offley Arms, the name reflecting a local landowning family in previous centuries, is open from 11.30 until 2.30pm at lunchtimes and from 5.30pm on Mondays to Saturdays. Usual Sunday hours.

## Madeley

Standing on slightly higher ground the sandstone church of Madeley overlooks the older part of this now large village. The site was most probably occupied since early Saxon times but the church we see today is very much Victorian restoration of an earlier structure. The core of the village nestled around the pool and dam of the river Lea, looks delightful at any time of the year and particularly on a frosty spring morning when the sun begins to rise.

*The Pool, Madeley*

This walk is based on footpath routes cleared with the assistance of Newcastle-under-Lyme borough council and several local walks are written up in an excellent booklet prepared by George Riley. It is available at local Tourist Information Centres and offers several walks in the Madeley area.

# The Walk

(1) From the car park entrance, turn right to pass by the entrance of the old vicarage and then by cottages to a road junction where you turn left along a road known as The Holborn to the main road. Cross over to walk along the pavement by the pool, passing Old Hall on the opposite side, a magnificent seventeenth century building with an inscription "Walk knave. Waht's lookest at". This is thought to been a message dating from the English Civil War to fool local Parliamentarians into thinking that the owners were loyal while in reality they were Royalist

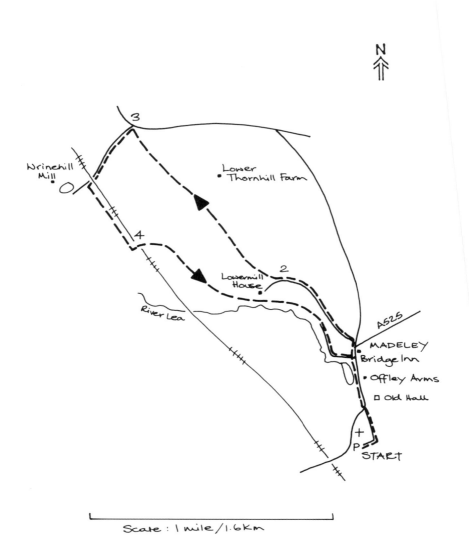

*The Offley Arms*

supporters. Pass by the Offley Arms and Bridge Inn, both renovated in recent years. Then, turn left after the village stores into Furnace Lane, the name reflecting small scale industries that once thrived here in the last century but exist no longer. Follow this route out of the village.

(2) As the road bears left towards Lower Mill house cross a stile by a gate thus keeping ahead. Keep company with the hedge on the right up to the scar of an old working and then just after as the field rises, bear slightly left towards a stile in the opposite hedge. Once over, bear right and follow the hedge on your right until a corner where there is an electric telegraph pole. The farm over fields to your right is Lower Thornhill. Bear slightly left across the field, almost following the line of poles to a stile at the bottom of a bank in the far left bottom corner, a stile which cannot be seen until close up. Cross it and head for the house on the right of the three, on the other side of this very large field.

(3) Cross a stile and go left·along the lane by the houses to pass under the railway and then look for a stile on the left before the entrance to the old Wrinehill mill which has been a mill of some description throughout the ages. Follow the embankment, passing through a gateway and then cross the railway by way of a brick bridge, a section of railway route which has seen many a speed trial in the years of steam.

(4) In the next field a stile can be seen to the right but a barbed wire fence obstructs the path. However, it is easy to walk along a track to the right and then cut left to join the stile. From this point, head slightly right across another large field with no real landmarks to look for. As a hedge is approached, look for a waymarked stile mid-field.

Cross the stile and keep ahead again along a slightly sunken green path to a mound and just below it on the right is a double stile leading down into a little pasture by the River Lea. Bear slightly left to walk along the field's edge and beneath houses to join a path alongside an old water channel. Cross a stile to walk through a wet patch and then along a fenced path by the water works. The route follows it around to the right by the works, over the bridge and then up the track to a road by the new Mews and the old mill. Turn left into Madeley and right at the main junction to return to the church.

# 14. OAKAMOOR

**Route:** Oakamoor – Moss's Bank – Dimmings Dale – Ramblers Retreat – Farley – Oakamoor

**Distance:** 4 miles

**Map:** O.S. Pathfinder 810 Ashbourne and Churnet Valley.

**Start:** Picnic Site, Oakamoor (Grid Reference 053447)

**Access:** There is a limited bus service to Oakamoor on Mondays to Saturdays. Check with Staffordshire Bus for details on (0785) 223344.

*By Car* – car travellers should make their way to Cheadle on the A52 and A522. Then take the B5417 road to Oakamoor. There is ample parking at the picnic site.

## The Lord Nelson Hotel (0538) 702242

This homely little public house stands in the middle of the village, just off the road to Whiston. According to the Fourth Edition of "Real Ale In and Around The Potteries" this 18th century house was once owned by the PHRA or The Peoples Refreshment House Association and served Kimberley Ales from Hardys and Hansons in Nottinghamshire. There's a snug lounge and homely bar, appropriately adorned with reminders of one of the nation's heroes – Lord Nelson – where the thirsty rambler can now try a pint of Worthington or Bass draught beer. This traditional pub also offers food during all sessions.

The Lord Nelson is open from noon until 4pm on Mondays to Saturdays and from 7pm in the evening. Usual Sunday hours. Families are welcome and there is a seating area to the front and a garden.

## Oakamoor

Walking in the Churnet valley never disappoints. Whatever the weather or season, it has a variety of landscapes that appeal to the eye. So it was with our Victorian ancestors for Alton became fashionable as a place to stay awhile and was soon dubbed "Little Switzerland", because of its Alpine features – though on a smaller scale. Parts of the valley, however, became a hotbed of local industrialisation – quarrying, forging and smelting. Oakamoor was the original site of Thomas Boltons Copper Works, which is now at Froghall. It is said that the works produced most of the copper wire for the first trans Atlantic underwater cable, some 20,000 miles in total.

Much of the earlier industrial developments are now gone, buildings overgrown or put to another use. The same has happened to some of the parkland, Alton Towers theme park being the prime example. This 4 mile ramble allows the walker to enjoy the richness of the Churnet valley within such a short distance.

*The Lord Nelson, Oakamoor*

# The Walk

(1) Start from the car park and picnic site at Oakamoor, which happens to be on the site of old works too. Turn left onto the road and pass by the old station building, now a private residence but unmistakingly exhibiting a North Staffordshire Railway identity. In approximately one quarter of a mile go left at the road junction but not far along go right before a wall. The climbing begins in earnest as the path leads up through the deciduous woodland of Moss's Banks.

(2) Towards the top a house comes into view. This is not your way, so be sure to look for a right turning by a rhododendron bush which leads to a gate to the right of the house. Go through this and follow the track as it curves around to a pond. Pass by it to then cross a track and go through another gate. Keep ahead now for a short distance to Dimmingsdale Youth hostel. Beforehand look out for an old boundary stone on the right.

Pass to the right of the youth hostel buildings, go through a gap-stile and keep ahead, with views through the woodland to Alton. The path begins to descend as another gap-stile is approached and then drops down to a wider path leading left at first but then plunging right to the ponds in the valley bottom, pools which once would have stored water to power a mill below.

(3) Follow the well-worn path on the left down Dimmingsdale. It curves left, then crosses a bridge before meeting another main track by a house at Earl's Rock. Go right and continue down Ousal Dale to The Ramblers Retreat, a place of refreshment mid way on the ramble. At the road go virtually straight across onto a track which crosses Lord's Bridge over the River Churnet. The path curves left and then right to climb up Barbary Gutter to the characterful old Park Lodge. There is an uncanny feeling as shrieks and cries of people on the rides of Alton Towers are heard.

(4) You might well be tempted by the fun but your way is to turn left by a gatehouse and then almost immediately right over a stile by a gate. Keep ahead across Farley Park to cross a stile and ahead between trees to cross another. Parkhouse farm comes closer as the path descends the

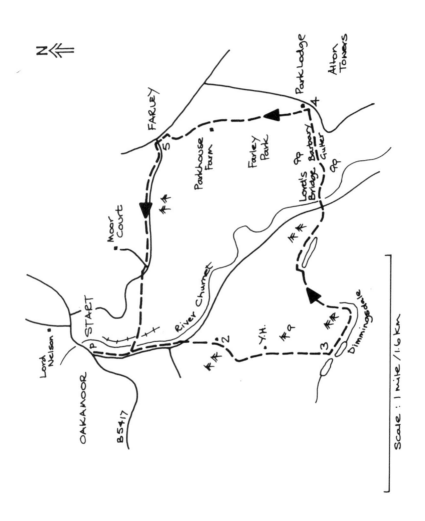

bank to a gateway. Go ahead, keeping company with a fence on the right, to another gate by a lane. Cross this and follow the little path leading slightly left between young trees to cross another stile. In the next field head slightly left up to the top left-hand corner. The path crosses a stile and is hemmed between fences to the road at Farley.

(5) Turn left and then turn next left along a road signposted to Oakamoor. The road descends gently and after the turning to Moor Court on the right, look for a gap-stile on the left at the next corner opposite South Lodge. Head slightly right across the field to a stream and just to the right of a line of trees. Near the garden fence bear slightly left to soon meet a stile by a gateway. Keep ahead, cross the track and continue slightly right down the hill to join a hedge on the right leading to a gap. Go through it and turn right onto a path leading to the old railway track where you turn right. Cross the railway bridge and at the road turn right to retrace steps to Oakamoor.

# 15. LONGPORT to STOKE-ON-TRENT

**Route:** Longport Railway Station – Trent and Mersey Canal at Middleport – Etruria – Stoke-on-Trent

**Distance:** 4 miles

**Map:** O.S. Pathfinder 809 Stoke-on-Trent

**Start:** Longport Railway Station (Grid Reference 856494).

**Access:** This is a linear walk. We suggest that you catch a train from Stoke station to Longport and walk back to the Blacks Head for, once settled, it is difficult to prise yourself away for a walk from this pub. Those wishing to start from Burslem, to incorporate the Bulls Head, might like to catch the China Link (hourly link around the Pottery Shops) to Burslem town centre from Stoke station or Hanley.

## The Black's Head (0782) 415594

This enterprising free house in North Street, a little distance from Stoke centre, has been for the past few years a haven for those who enjoy a good range of beers in traditional but comfortable bars. The owner has introduced his own brew known as "Roaches Best Ale" also stocking a continuously changing range of brews. The two rooms are served from a central bar by congenial staff and food is served at lunchtimes until approximately 2 pm, although rolls are available at most times. The Black's Head is open from noon until 3pm (4pm on Saturdays) at lunchtimes and from 5.30pm in the evenings except Saturday when it re opens at 7pm. Usual Sunday hours prevail. The pub is not geared up for families but does have a small area away from the bar to the rear of the hostelry. It is a pleasant place to finish a walk of an evening, and visitors are made genuinely  welcome.

# The Bull's Head, Burslem (0782 834153)

No book worth its salt would omit the Potteries very own brewery which began in the mid-1980s. Named in honour of the Titanic's master, Captain Smith from Burslem, the brewery has at long last its own brewery tap in the township. Ironically, it was reopened on April 13th, 1992 the 80th anniversary of the tragic maiden voyage. The two roomed pub is served by a central bar which offers a selection from the brewery range – Best Bitter, Lifeboat, Premium, Captain Smith's Strong Ale and Wreckage (Original Gravity of 1080 so handle with caution). The pub also has a policy of offering guest beers from other small independent breweries rather than those associated with the brewing giants. There are a number of traditional features here such as bar skittles, and several wall pictures and adornments like the traditional hop sack from Canon Frome in Herefordshire. The only regret the authors have is that Titanic ales are not more widely available in The Potteries.

The Bull's Head is open from 11.30 until 3pm and from 5.30pm Mondays through to Thursdays, all day on Fridays and on Saturdays 11.30am until 3 pm, re-opening at 6.30 pm. Usual Sunday hours. Rolls are available.

*Bottle Oven at Price and Kensington*

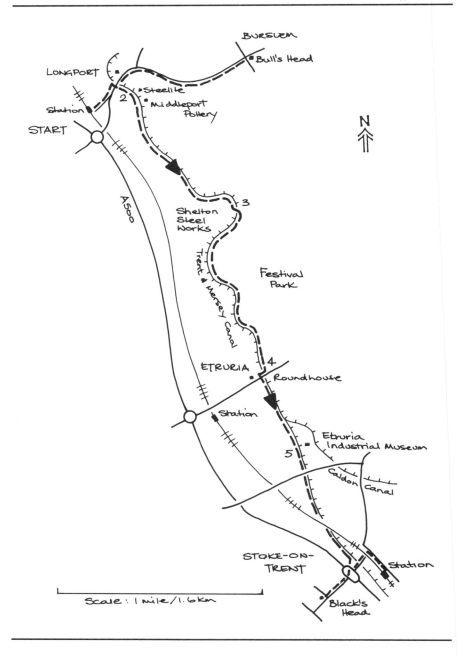

# The Walk

(1) Start from Longport Railway Station by crossing the footbridge and walking along Station Road to the main road. (Those joining from Burslem should walk down the main road, Newcastle Road,for the best part of a mile to Trubshaw Cross and bear left to the canal where The Packhorse is on your right. Turn left and enter the canal towpath by way of Canal Street to the left of The Packhorse public house which stands almost opposite The Duke of Bridgewater. Ahead is Price and Kensington, well known to many for their manufacture of teapots. Like so many pottery manufacturers along the canal they have retained old buildings of character, including a bottle oven here. This makes the walk so attractive. It also evokes mixed feelings for several canal-side buildings stand in a poor state of repair, while other sites, such as The Roundhouse in the grounds of the Evening Sentinel complex or the Etruscan Industrial Museum exhibit innovative restoration work.

(2) The towpath curves right to pass Steelite and then the Middleport Pottery, a superb example of a Victorian pottery complete with wharf

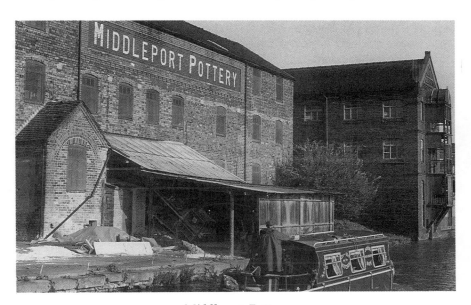

*Middleport Pottery*

and crane where raw materials would have been brought in and wares despatched by boat. Continue ahead by several fascinating buildings to reach the Shelton steel works, still a considerable size but a shadow of its former self. The canal winds around to the right to the noise of hard steel rolling out and trains struggling along worn tracks in contrast to the still waters of the canal. On the opposite bank is the wooded landscape of Festival Park, one of the sites chosen as a Garden Festival and now dominated by leisure activities including a dry ski slope. The towpath dips beneath the overhang of one of the main sheds.

(3) The towpath is now on the left of the canal and passes a boat-yard on the left. Climb to the main road at Etruria. Turn right and drop back down by The Roundhouse, one of the few remaining buildings from the old Wedgwood works. It now houses artefacts reflecting the importance of Wedgwood in the area and a newspaper and printing museum. It is difficult to believe that this was the site of a model village established by Josiah Wedgwood in 1769. To the left is the only other remnant, Etruria Hall, which stands linked to The Moat House Hotel. Wedgwood lived at the hall during the late 1760s and 1770s and the surrounding area was soon covered with houses for the workers in his factory. It was Wedgwood among others who encouraged the building of the canal to enhance prospects of trade. Wedgwood cut the very first sod in 1766. He could have scarcely believed that a steel works would have flattened his empire after the departure of the main Wedgwood plant to Barlaston in the 1930s.

(4) On the towpath turn right to walk under the bridge and ahead for the junction of the Caldon Canal at Summit Lock. The Caldon was James Brindley's last triumph. He did not live to see its completion for he succumbed to pneumonia following a drenching when surveying the navigation. A statue standing on the opposite bank celebrates his great engineering skills. Just below the locks is the Etruria Industrial Museum which houses Britain's sole surviving steam-powered Potters Mill, including an 1820s beam engine.

(5) Continue along the Trent and Mersey Canal to more bottle ovens behind the Twyford's Factory and the cemetery on the other bank. The towpath descends into a dank darkness beneath the railway and passes by Stoke Lock. Look for gates on the right to exit here to the middle of the roundabout. Not an inspiring introduction to Stoke-on-Trent but a

speedy walk to the right through the graffiti ridden underpass brings you to the Shelton Road. The Black's Head is in North Street a little way up on the right,a place to repair awhile before your journey home. If you started the walk in Burslem, the bus stop before the corner of North Street provides a very frequent direct bus service, but be sure to call into the Black's Head beforehand if you enjoy a well-kept pint of real ale.

# *16. MAYFIELD*

**Route:** Hanging Bridge – Upper Mayfield – Okeover Bridge – Mapleton – Hanging Bridge

**Distance:** 4 miles

**Map:** O.S. Pathfinder 810 Ashbourne and Churnet Valley

**Start:** From the Hanging Bridge on the main A52 road. (Grid Reference: 158457)

**Access:** The Hanging Bridge at Mayfield is served by a daily Manchester to Derby bus and a Mondays to Saturdays service from Uttoxeter to Ashbourne.

*By Car* – Travel on the A52 to the junction with the B5032 road to Mayfield and Uttoxeter. There is limited on street parking in Mayfield but please park considerately.

## The Okeover Arms (0335) 29305

The Okeover Arms, named after the Okeovers from nearby Okeover Hall was intially a public house but changed to a temperance hotel in the 1920s. It remained dry until 1962 when it was converted back to a public house and remains as such to this day. There is a lounge cum restaurant area and a bar, the latter used mainly by walkers. This often has a fire blazing of a Winter's day and many guests sit back to treasure the delightful old photographs of the village and Ashbourne, several of which date from the latter part of the last century. There's also a pictorial reminder of the Shrovetide football match held each year in Ashbourne, no ordinary match but one where the ball is mauled up and down the town by very large opposing teams who hail from the southern or northern side of the town. A rather messy affair at the best of times.

The Okeover sells a cracking pint of Burton Ale on handpump and offers food until 2.30 p.m. at lunch and 10.00 p.m. in the evening. Opening times are from 11.30 a.m. until 3.00 p.m. on Mondays to Saturday lunchtimes and from 7.00 p.m. in the evening. Families are welcome in the first room on the left from the car park entrance and there is a garden to the rear of the car park. The landlord and landlady stress that walkers are most welcome but please kick your boots off at the door! While mentioning doors there is a resident ghost which walks regularly from the old front door to the old back door. Both are now bricked up but that's of little consequence!

*Okeover Hall*

## Mayfield

The very north-eastern tip of Staffordshire, near to the historic market town of Ashbourne, offers fine walking for the rambler. The village of Mayfield very much reflects the different ages of industrial development. There are working mills on the river surrounded by tightly packed houses built to house the workforce. In contrast, not half a mile away on the rising slopes, are older cottages and houses dating from when agriculture and home-based weaving dominated. The transformation from a rural economy to a more industrialised society is a theme embroidered by George Eliot into her novel, Adam Bede, some of the material for the book having been derived from this area.

## Mapleton

Some pronounce this as "Mappleton". It's a little Derbyshire village on a spring line above the banks of the River Dove. It is fortunate in retaining its pub, shop and church. The latter is a distinctive-looking place of worship cherished by the local community.

*Mapleton Church*

# The Walk

(1) At the junction between the A52 and the B5032 roads at The Hanging Bridge; the name refers to the handsome arches spanning the silvery waters of the River Dove, rather than a place of public executions. Cross the bridge to walk up a narrower road rising to the left of the Queens Arms. Another road joins it from the left in Upper Mayfield. Turn right to dip down to the main A52 road where care should be taken to cross here.

(2) Walk a few paces down the hill to cross the road and turn left along a track which is a little overgrown at this time of year. The track bends right into a field, past an old farm building, and running ahead with a hedge to the right.

(3) On the hillside to the left are earthworks known as strip lynchets, an early form of farming hillsides using terraces, almost in vineyard fashion. The track deteriorates to a path at the next gate where there is a stone gap-stile alongside. Go through it and keep ahead again to come to a wooden stile by a small gate. Cross the access track to Throstle Nest farm and head slightly right to the opposite corner of the field where you go through the barred gate to exit onto a road known as Birdsgrove Lane.

(4) Turn left and soon enter Okeover Park (which is private). Between the ancient oaks can be seen the ancestral home of the Okeover family, one of the few houses in the country to have been passed continuously between heirs from the 12th to the 20th. The house has been modified considerably through the ages and the little church nearby was restored in the 1850s.

(5) At the junction turn right to cross the singled arched bridge over the River Dove into Derbyshire. Look for a gap-stile on the right and cut through the field to the distinctive looking Mapleton church. Go right to pass The Okeover Arms.

(6) Leave the village and as the road rises to the left into woodland, keep ahead through a gateway and down a track into the flood plain of the river. Go through another gateway and bear slightly right to a field

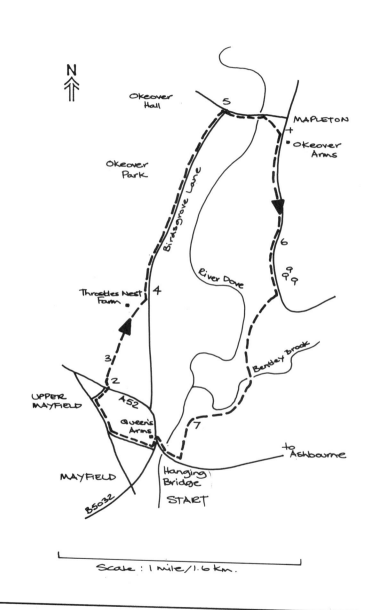

corner. Proceed in a similar direction to a stile by a gate, coming closer to the tree lined river bank which is to your right. Go through a narrow gap-stile by wire fencing and then turn left to follow a hedge to a footbridge over the Bentley Brook. Cross here and bear right along the stream, through two gaps, the latter with wire fencing. Walk ahead to the stile on the embankment, a defence against flooding. Once over, go right and cross the fencing.

You soon reach the end of the embankment. Be sure to cross the gap-stile on the left (marked with a white footpath sign) rather than the wooden stile beyond which is not the right of way.

(7) The path keeps company with the hedge on the right, through a gap and ahead, again, to a wooden stile, which leads onto a drive by a public house which was being refurbished at the time of writing. Walk to the main road and turn right to cross The Hanging Bridge.

# 17. BETLEY

**Route:** Betley – Church Lane – Cooksgate – Shraleybrook – Cooksgate – Adderley Green – Betley

**Distance:** 6 miles

**Map:** O.S. Pathfinder 808 Audlem

**Start:** Betley Church (Grid Reference: SJ 756486)

**Access:** Betley has a daily bus service from Hanley and Crewe. Contact Staffordshire Busline for details on (0785) 223344

*By Car* – the A525 from Newcastle-under-Lyme then the A531. There is limited on street parking in Betley

---

## The Rising Sun Inn, Shraleybrook (0782) 720600

The Rising Sun began brewing in 1990, supplying a number of North Staffordshire free trade outlets as well as the Rising Sun Inn. The homely pub with a large L shaped lounge and smaller bar cum games area offers an amazing number of beers for the weary rambler to sample. The breweries own range includes Mild, Sunlight, Rising, Setting and Sunstroke, the names adequately describing the potency of each brew. Those wishing to terminate the walk here might care to sip a glass of Total Eclipse which has an Original Gravity of 1072! The Rising Sun Inn also has a policy of offering other breweries guest beers so one might find such names as Burton Bridge, Woods or Smiles on offer too.

The Rising Sun Inn is open from noon until 3.30pm Mondays to Fridays and from 6.30pm in the evening. It is open all day on Saturdays and usual Sunday hours are observed. Families are welcome and there is a beer garden. Food is served from noon until 2.20pm at lunchtimes and to 10pm in the evenings.

*The Rising Sun, Shraleybrook*

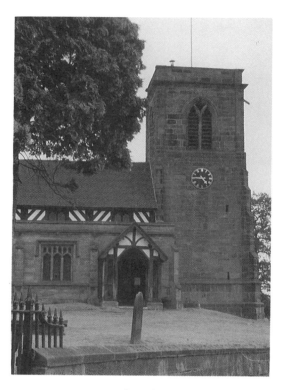

*Betley Church*

## Betley

The lovely village of Betley, which straddles the old road from Newcastle to Crewe, has many fine houses including Betley Court dating from the 18th century and the half-timbered Betley Old Hall. Betley church dates from the 12th century but has been restored throughout the centuries. It is noted for its extensive surviving woodwork and monuments dedicated to local notable families, the Fletchers and Fletchers-Twemlows. Near to the village is Cracow Moss and Betley Mere, described as a low lying wet land area rich in wildlife. There are several delightful walks from Betley written up by George Riley, published as a booklet by Newcastle-under-Lyme Borough Council and available from local tourist information offices.

# The Walk

(1) From the main road in Betley, Church Lane curves right and then left to pass by the church and into countryside. Follow the lane for just under one mile by Yewtree Cottage, Fields farm and Cooksgate where Church lane meets Heighley Lane.

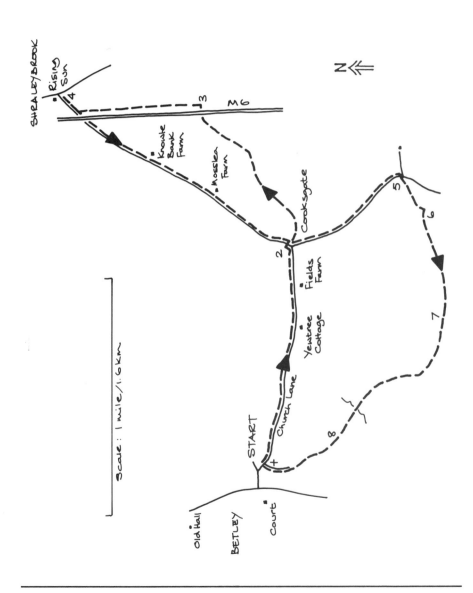

SCALE: 1 mile/1.6 km

(2) Keep to the left fork but as this begins to bend to the left look for a stile inset into the hedge on the right. There is a small pool hidden away on the right which is home for a gaggle of geese and wildfowl from time to time.

Once over the stile proceed ahead, but move closer to the hedge on the left. Follow this as it curves left and then cross a stile into the next field. Go straight on to cross another stile by a gate but half way along this next field cut right down to the bottom corner by the wood, with the motorway now becoming more visible and certainly more audible.

Cross the stile and keep ahead in the next field to a five barred gate where an adjacent stile is crossed. A tractor track bears left but you head slightly right across the pasture to a tunnel under the motorway. Go through this.

(3) The other side of the motorway is no less noisy. Turn left and follow the boundary path to cross a footbridge then through fields, very often in cereal crop to exit onto Knowlbank Road and your effort is rewarded by turning right to one of England's rare home brew pubs, The Rising Sun at Shraleybrook.

(4) From The Rising Sun, make your way back up Knowlbank Road, under the motorway and then the lane reverts to a quiet country thoroughfare again. Pass Knowlbank and Moss Lea farms before descending to Cooksgate again. Go left at the junction to climb up to Adderley Green by way of Hillside and Heighley farms.

(5) At Adderley Green look for a stile on the right almost opposite the T-junction. Cross the stile and enter the field. Climb the bank beneath old oaks. There is evidence of an old hedge here and possibly a track at one time. The path rises to cross a stile in the top corner of the enclosure where you can enjoy good views of North Staffordshire. Keep ahead with the hedge to your left but at the next corner turn left over the stile to another within a matter of paces. Cross this and bear right to find yet another stile. Cross this and walk ahead over the summit by the edge of old workings to enter a large field.

(6) Follow the boundary hedge on the left down to the far bottom corner where a stile ahead (rather than the one on the left) is crossed. Keep

company again with the hedge on the left but look for a stile on the left part way down the field. Cross it, turn right then cross a double stile ahead before climbing up the bank now with a tall, thick set hedge to your right.

(7) As the field begins to descend, cross a stile on the right between holly bushes, turn left and then within a few paces strike out across the field to cut the corner in the direction of a stile in the bottom hedge. Do not cross it; instead, keep ahead along the hedgerow to cross a stile and sleeper bridge. Then bear slightly right across the field in the direction of a house in the distance. There are two stiles here as paths meet at this field corner. Choose the one on the left which means climbing a small bank into a field. Go straight on over the brow and then dip down to a stile. Cross it and step gingerly down to the bridge over the brook. Climb the steps into the field and then keep ahead. The path rises to cross a stile beneath an oak tree.

(8) Walk ahead over a slight brow in the field to cross a stile, then proceeding ahead to a stile which leads to the corner of Betley's cricket ground. Walk by the club house to exit along a track by Betley church, the railings dating from 1856. Keep ahead at the junction and retrace your steps back to the main road.

# 18. KINGSLEY

**Route:** Kingsley – Hazlescross – Consall Forge – Cherryeye Bridge – Kingsley

**Distance:** 3 miles

**Start:** Kingsley Church (Grid Reference: 013469)

**Map:** O.S. Pathfinder 810 Ashbourne and Churnet Valley

**Access:** Kingsley enjoys a Mondays to Saturdays bus service. Telephone Staffordshire Busline on (0785) 223344 for details.

*By Car* – The village main A52 road from The Potteries. There is limited car parking near to the church.

## The Black Lion, Consall Forge (0538) 550294

The Black Lion, built to serve the canal trade, is a remarkable survivor, Until recent years access by road was discouraged and most people came on foot or boat. This tradition continues during the Summer months when the Caldon Canal attracts quite few boats aiming for Froghall Wharf terminus.

The Black Lion has two rooms, a bar and a separate room often used by those eating. There is also a large outside drinking area stretching down to the canal-side. Cask conditioned Ruddles County and Marstons Pedigree are on offer and food is served at lunch until 2.30pm and in the evening until 9pm. Opening hours are 11am until 3pm and from 6pm on Mondays to Saturdays. Usual Sunday hours. Families are welcome at this lovely old canal-side pub. This must be a compulsory stop!

## Kingsley

The large hillside church of St Werburgh with its fine medieval tower is renowned locally for its bell-ringing. The churchyard with several very old gravestones, a veritable social history of the area. Kingsley was once a small scale mining community as well as engaging in agriculture.

*The Black Lion, Consall Forge*

## Consall Forge

Consall Forge was also far more industrial in previous times than now. There were several lime kilns and local small scale quarries in the area and much of the material was shipped out from a small wharf along the Caldon Canal. Fortunately, several kilns survive and are near to the Black Lion, although not kept in a tidy state when the authors passed by.

# The Walk

(1) Start from the road by the church. Go through a small gate on the left leading through the churchyard to two kissing gates in the far right corner with a track and farm to your right. Once in the field go left and follow the field's edge to another stile and step down. Leave the Staffordshire Way here (which is signposted right).

(2) You continue ahead through this field to go through a stile, now moving away from the village seen across fields on the left. Head slightly right in the next field to a stile at the next boundary. Once over walk in a similar direction to join a slight track by an old scar on the right. The track leads down to a gateway and exits by way of a cottage into the hamlet of Hazlescross.

(3) Go left and at the junction bear right. The road curves left to another hamlet, Hazles, where you turn right, as signposted, down a well-worn path at Far Kingsley Banks. This winds down, quite steeply in places, to a junction in the lower woodland section. Turn right here and follow the path down to a footbridge, across the railway and then left along a track to the towpath above old Consall Flint Mill. Turn left along the towpath for The Black Lion.

(4) Retrace your steps along the towpath under the railway, which then happens to be squeezed between the canal and river along the next section. The small platform shelter seen on the right at Consall Forge halt is maintained by a group of enthusiasts who worship the day when a steam hauled passenger service is restored. An early guide described the route as one of the most picturesque lines in England and many

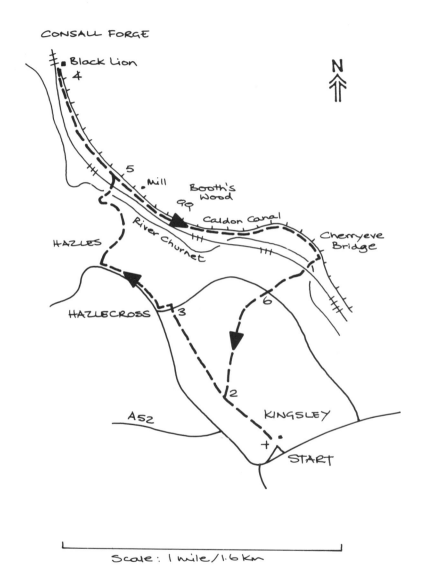

CONSALL FORGE

Black Lion
4

5
Mill
Booth's
Wood
qq
Caldon Canal
River Churnet
HAZLES
Cherryeve
Bridge
HAZLECROSS 3
6
2
A52
KINGSLEY
START

Scale: 1 mile/1.6 km

curse the day when British Rail closed it to passenger traffic in the 1960s. It would be good to see part of the track converted to an off-road cycle route, too.

(5) The route then follows the canal to the old Consall flint mill passing by a small pottery *en route*. The path   passes beneath Booth's Wood where the smell of wild garlic pervades the valley in springtime. The towpath comes to Cherryeye Bridge, a tight bridge for navigators and then 300 metres beyond look for a stile on the right. The path crosses the river and then sweeps under the railway to very shortly rise to the right through wet ground to a stile which exits onto Banks Lane.

(6) Cross the road and then climb steps up the steep hillside, with a falconry to the right. It comes to a stile at the top of the wood. The path continues ahead to a stile in the next boundary and then through the next field in a similar direction to a gap-stile by a barred gate. Go through this and head slightly left to the top far left corner. Go over the steps and stile and walk ahead to a gate before a farm. Do not go through but instead cut right through a kissing gate into the churchyard. Turn left to retrace your steps to the road.

# 19. WATERHOUSES

**Route:** Waterhouses – Cauldon – Yew Tree Inn – Duke's Lane – Waterfall Cross – Waterfall – Waterhouses

**Distance:** 5 miles

**Map:** O.S. Outdoor Leisure 24 – The White Peak and Pathfinder 810 – Ashbourne and the Churnet Valley

**Start:** Car Park at Waterhouses old railway station (Grid Reference: 085502)

**Access:** The 201 Derby to Manchester bus serves Waterhouses daily.

*By Car* – The car park is signposted in the village on the A523 road between Leek and Ashbourne.

## The Yew Tree Inn (0538) 308348

This must be one of the most unusual pubs in the country, featured in The Good Beer Guide year after year. The landlord and landlady have collected an amazing collection of polyphonia and pianola, clocks and other fascinating artefacts. The separate areas of the pub are served from a circular bar. M&B Mild, Draught Bass and Burton Bridge Bitter are on hand-pull and invariably found in excellent condition.

The pub also retains a bar skittles table and darts. Food is available always and families are welcome. The Yew Tree is open from 10am in the morning until 3pm Monday to Saturday lunchtimes and from 6pm in the evenings. Usual Sunday Hours. It is a marvellous pub which the authors thoroughly recommend to you.

## Waterhouses

The village straddles the River Hamps and is the gateway for those walking or cycling up the Manifold Valley to Hulme End. The North Staffordshire Railway terminated here and railway buildings are used as a cycle hire base now. The cutting of the first sod on the 3rd October 1899 must have been an occasion as it started as a luncheon and carried well on into the night! The line survives to the nearby Cauldon quarry but in mothballs and most commentators fear for its future as a freight link.

*Bar skittles at The Yew Tree*

# The Walk

(1) From the car park return to the wooden posts near the entrance and turn right down a little path to the Caldon Road. Go left under the bridge and then cross to join a fenced metalled path which winds its way through the works and quarrying. The path crosses a concrete bridge and soon afterwards becomes a track.

(2) The track reaches a junction. Take the right fork. The church is now to the left as your proceed ahead along a quiet road through the village

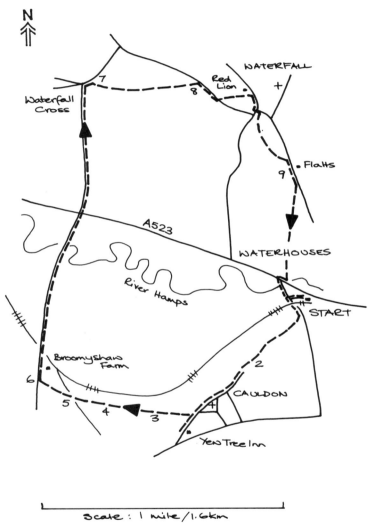

N

WATERFALL

Red Lion

7

8

Waterfall Cross

+

Flatts

9

A523

WATERHOUSES

River Hamps

START

Broomyshaw Farm

2

6

CAULDON

5

4

3

Yew Tree Inn

Scale : 1 mile/1.6km

of Cauldon. This leads to the Yew Tree Inn where a stop is obligatory. Suitably refreshed, retrace your steps but before the first cottage as the road curves right go left through a gate and then head slightly right down the field towards three electricity poles. Continue in a similar direction as the field dips and tapers.

(3) There should be a stile in the low level walling into a green lane thick with growth but as this is not clear the nearest way through is at the gateway a few metres down. Once through, walk down the bank where old steps can be found near to the stream. It is not possible to cross the stream here, so go a little upstream to paddle or stride an easier part. This section may be improved in due course.

(4) The old railway is to your right including a distinctive under-bridge. Your way is ahead, however, through wet ground to approach a low dry-stone wall on the left and groupings of three electricity poles on the right. The wall gives way to the left but go straight on moving closer to another railway line now seen more clearly on the left. Look for a stile standing beneath a cluster of trees. Cross it and then proceed over the line to a gate on the other side.

(5) Go slightly right from the embankment to pass through a gate. Continue ahead in a similar direction passing a line of trees then a wooden stile. The farm in the foreground is Broomyshaw. Your way is to head slightly left up the field dipping but then rising to a stone gap-stile beyond the electric telegraph pole.

(6) Enter Duke's Lane and turn right to follow the lane past the farm, over the railway and through to the main A523 road. Cross the main road and walk up the hill to the isolated farmsteads at Waterfall Cross, an ancient meeting place of tracks. Go right at the triangular junction and at the brow of the hill just beyond right through a gateway. While the path is not clear on the ground it is signposted.

(7) Head slightly left across the field to a gateway just to the right of the field corner. Then proceed in a similar direction in the next two fields to a composite wood and stone gap-stile. Go slightly left again down the dip to a stone gap-stile well to the right of the trees but keeping to the left of the main gully. Go through the upper reaches of it, making your way slightly left towards the line of trees which form a truncated hedge.

Look for the stile at the end of the trees. Cross this and go right to a stile by a gate which exits onto a road.

(8) Turn right and walk approximately 200 paces to find a stile on the left. Keep ahead, crossing two stiles, to descend to the road by The Red Lion public house. Turn right to reach a junction. Turn left and opposite the cottages go right through a gap-stile (as signposted) and ahead to another gap-stile in a field boundary. Then set a course in a similar direction through several narrow enclosures. Originally, the path was delineated by a series of low level stone gap-stiles, some of which remain, others have collapsed. You eventually come to a gateway. Walk ahead in the same direction to a large gap-stile hidden in a thick set hedge. Go through it.

(9) Go right and follow the lane down past the entrance to Flatts. Just beyond, go right through a gap-stile by a gate and head slightly left down the field to cross a wooden stile and ahead by an old tree to a gap-stile by a collapsed wall. Continue ahead in the same direction towards Waterhouses through narrow pastures and stiles, keeping to the right of a small hut. Then follow the well-used path across the final field to Waterhouses. The path exits by a gate onto the main road. Go left and then right at Ye Old Crown public house.

# 20. STANLEY

**Route:** Stanley – Acres Barn – Cats Edge – Caldon Canal – Stanley Moss – Stanley Pool – Bagnall – Stanley Pool – Stanley

**Distance:** 7 miles

**Map:** O.S. Pathfinder 792 Kidsgrove and Leek

**Start:** The Travellers Rest, Stanley (Grid Reference: 933523)

**Access:** The PMT bus company runs an hourly service from Hanley. Contact PMT for details on (0782) 747000

*By Car* – Turn right off the A53 at Stockton Brook to Stanley Moor and Bagnall. There is limited on-street car parking in the village.

## The Travellers Rest, Stanley Village (0782) 502580

The Travellers Rest is a characterful looking pub set among cottages in the middle of Stanley. The range of draught beers includes Martons Burton Bitter and Pedigree and Aylesbury Bitter (brewed at Ind Coope, Burton upon Trent). The Travellers Rest is open from noon until 2.30pm at lunchtimes and from 7pm in the evenings. Sunday normal hours. Food is available until 2pm in the afternoon and until 9.30pm in the evenings. Families are welcome but not Saturday evenings when the pub is unable to cater for children. There is an outdoor area.

## The Stafford Arms, Bagnall (0782) 502266

The Stafford Arms was known earlier in the last century as the Kings Arms and changed to The Marquis of Stafford in 1879. A central bar serves many nooks and crannies and there's a lovely fireplace in this warm hostelry. The pub has on hand-pull Draught Bass, Tetley Bitter and usually one other guest beer. It is open from noon until 3pm and from 7pm in the evening (although this is often earlier in the Summer at 6.30 pm). Food is served until 2pm at lunch and until 9.30pm in the evening. Families are welcome and there is an outdoor area. This is a friendly pub with a lively atmosphere.

*The Traveller's Rest, Stanley*

# Stanley

Above the valley of the Endon Brook, just to the north of the City, is the delightful hillside village of Stanley. Local people suggest that the name comes from the aristocratic Stanley family, the Earls of Derby, although it is possible that it is a corruption of the old English phrase "stone legh" meaning stone-laden ground. This 3 to 4 mile walk is easy going with only one or two climbs back up to the village.

*The Dam, Stanley Pool*

# Bagnall

Bagnall also seems a world removed from the bustle of The Potteries. The village green with shop, post office and church at opposite corners is a reminder of the traditional layout of many a rural settlement in North Staffordshire before the encroachment of modern development. Local historians suggest that Bagnall would have been called Bagga in Anglo

Saxon times, hence the derivation of its current name and a reflection of its antiquity. Look at the old cross flanked by five trees, planted early in the century to commemorate Queen Victoria's Diamond Jubilee, June 22, 1897. Beyond is Bagnall Hall, a seventeenth century building of great character. There is an excellent little history of the area published by the Bagnall Local History Group (1990) which is worth a read. It is available at bookshops.

*Old Cross, Bagnall*

# The Walk

(1) Start from outside The Travellers Rest pub at Stanley. Turn left to walk up the road climbing gently out of the village. The road then descends a little before rising again as it approaches a large stone farmhouse on the left. Almost immediately beyond is a track on the left leading to a farm known as Acres Barn. Go down here and a bridle gate

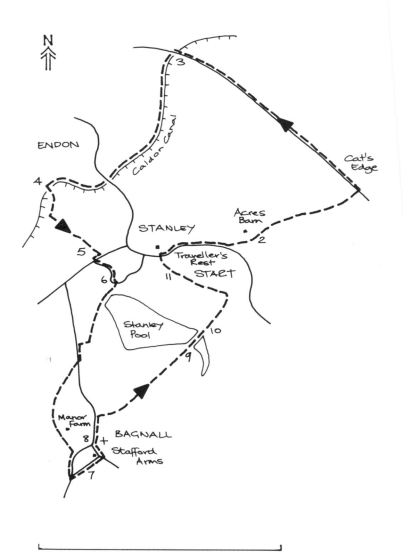

can seen to the right. However, a notice advises walkers to continue along the track towards the farm. Beforehand, turn right to go through a large five-barred gate into the field on the right. Once through walk ahead for a few metres to a bridle gate on the left. Go through it, thus rejoining the route.

(2) The bridleway is easy to follow (and is waymarked) through two more gates and across a footbridge. The next gate leads into a large field where the path keeps company with the hedge on the right. There are good views along this section towards Endon. The path continues through a gateway and then to a stile by a gate which leads onto a minor road near Cat's Edge. Go left and follow the road for approximately one mile, passing historic farmhouses on the way, as you descend to the Caldon Canal.

(3) Go over the stile on the right, just beyond the canal bridge and walk down to the towpath. Bear right and walk under the bridge and by Endon water services. This canal, built to the specifications of John Rennie, is much loved by canal users for its distinctive architecture and surrounding landscape make it a rather special journey by boat. The canal towpath is followed to a bridge over the junction to the Endon basin.

(4) Once over, go left but then walk up the bank to the smaller over-bridge. Bear left to cross the bridge and leave the canal, passing between picnic tables to a gap-stile which brings you to a field. Keep ahead on the well-worn path towards the houses and then cross the footbridge to walk at the edge of the housing between a wire fence and hedge. This leads to a footbridge and into a field where horses, belonging to a riding school, often graze. Keep ahead with the fence to your left but as this curves left go straight on to a wooden gap-stile beneath an ash tree. Walk a few paces to another gap-stile in a dry stone wall and then follow the clear path through a swathe of grass to a gap-stile in a wall.

(5) Exit onto the road and turn right to pass an old mill complex, now a stone works, then turning first left into Puddy lane, with a tranquil mill pool fresh with yellow irises seen on the left. The narrow lane rises steeply in places to Stanley, passing by the dam of Stanley pool. This

was built as a reservoir to serve the Caldon canal in the 1840s and is now home to the North Staffs sailing club.

(6) Keep ahead up the track which runs to the right of the dam. By the house a path goes through a gap-stile on the right by a gate. The well-walked route curves left through rougher grass, moving away from the pool and soon comes to a drive. This continues by houses to a road. Turn left and pass by cottages and houses on the right. Go down the track to the right of them to a gap-stile which leads into a field. Head slightly left to skim the field corner and then climb in a similar direction beneath and then between enormous holly bushes, climbing up a bank to climb a broken wooden stile into the next field where a scar of old quarrying remains. Turn left up the bank and walk to the tractor track which can get very muddy. Go left here and follow this by Manor Farm and along a lane into Bagnall. Turn right and at the junction left into the village centre and Stafford Arms.

*The Stafford Arms*

(7) Turn left from the entrance of the Stafford Arms, to bear left at the end of the green. Pass by the church, built in the 1830s and extended in the 1880s. Over the entrance door, to the right of the restored churchyard cross reads the following simple message:

*"Tis the house of Prayer – Go In,*
*Tis the Christian's Home by Right,*
*Find some nook, Confess thy Sin,*
*And go forth in Jesus' Might"*

(8) Keep right at the junction and beyond a group of house on the right as the road curves left go through a gap-stile by a barred gate into a field as signposted. Follow the tall hedge down the field, through a gap-stile and ahead moving away from the hedge to cross another gap-stile in a dry-stone wall, towards Stanley Pool. Continue through a gateway with a single post and cross a stile leading onto an embankment by the pool.

(9) Prior to the building of the reservoir this valley had at least one corn mill in operation. It is said that Bagnall Mill and other buildings were severely damaged when a pool dam burst. Local scribes reported fish rotting in the hedgerows for weeks afterwards.

(10) The path crosses a landing slip and proceeds ahead between trees. It reaches a sleeper footbridge and a junction of paths. Turn left here to cross a stile and keep ahead through a field to a stone gap-stile and wooden stile in succession. Keep ahead alongside an old hedgerow lined with tall oaks until a gate is reached. Go through it and switch sides of the boundary now walking with a wall to your left.

(11) The path comes to the top left corner where you walk through a gap-stile. Walk ahead for a short distance at the rear of gardens to old stone steps. Cross these and go diagonally across the field to a gap-stile by a gate to enter Stanley.

# 21. CHEDDLETON

**Route:** Cheddleton – Bridge Cliffe – Lowerhouse Farm – Finneylane – Cheddleton Heath – Cheddleton

**Distance:** 4 miles

**Map:** O.S. Outdoor Leisure 24 The White Peak

**Start:** Cheddleton Railway Centre (Grid Reference: 982521)

**Access:** Cheddleton is well served by buses from Hanley, Leek, and Longton.

*By Car* – travel on the A520 road from Cellarhead to Leek. There is limited car parking near to the Railway Centre but please park considerately.

## The Black Lion (0538) 360628

Hidden away by the parish church up Hollow Lane is The Black Lion, a superb village local which also offers a warm welcome to the visitor. The one-roomed hostelry offers Marstons Burton Bitter, Pedigree and Banks's Mild on hand-pull from a cosy bar. Sandwiches are available at lunch. In earlier times those who proved a little naughty would have been put in the stocks opposite by a gateway to the churchyard. The Black Lion is open at lunchtimes from noon until 3 pm (4.30 pm on Saturdays) and from 7 pm in the evening. Usual Sunday hours. Families are welcome and there are seats outside.

## Cheddleton

The much enlarged village of Cheddleton is steeped in history, particularly the old quarter around the church which is known for its exceptional Victorian decoration and William Morris glass. This was one of four villages which engaged in a Village Enterprise scheme a few years back in partnership with the Business School at Staffordshire University. The aim was to develop tourism on a scale appropriate to the wishes of the community, illustrating best practice such as the award winning Glencote caravan site. The major attractions in the village are the Railway Centre at Cheddleton station and The Flint Mill. The Flint mill dates from the 18th century and flints would have been brought by canal from the south east to be ground for the ceramics industry in the Potteries. This delightful site tucked between canal and river is open to the public at any reasonable time, although the machinery and equipment are usually on display at busier times only.

The Railway Centre is home to many people who would like to see the re-instatement of a steam hauled train service down the Churnet Valley towards Oakamoor. The very distinctive station building at Cheddleton is attributed to Pugin, better known for designing the House of Commons in the last century. His work for the North Staffordshire Railway has to be some of the finest rural railway architecture in the country. The Centre is usually open on Sunday afternoons but also most afternoons in the summer when refreshments can be obtained. There are steam open days throughout the year.

*The Black Lion, Cheddleton*

# The Walk

(1) At the road junction by the Railway Centre with your back to the crossing gates go ahead at the juction along a green track for a matter of a few paces before turning right of cross a stile. Climb up the bank keeping company with the fence on your left to cross a stile by Bridge Cliffe Farm. Keep ahead to a gap-stile which leads onto a road.

*Butter Cross, Cheddleton*

(2) Cross the road and a stile to enter a field, then make your way ahead to a stile which is crossed. Go through a narrower field to cross another stile to find an isolated cross, possibly here to mark the convergence of routes in earlier centuries, as a butter cross for trading purposes or as a preaching cross. The cross is one of a number said to have existed around Cheddleton.

(3) Keep ahead up the field along a path which becomes a track, rising up to a gap-stile by a gate and onwards to the farm buildings of Lower House Farm. The path passes to the right of the buildings to a road. Turn right to climb past the entrance to Upper Ferneyhill Farm and a cross path signposted on either side of the road. Just beyond at the corner go right through a gateway and then left through a gap-stile. The

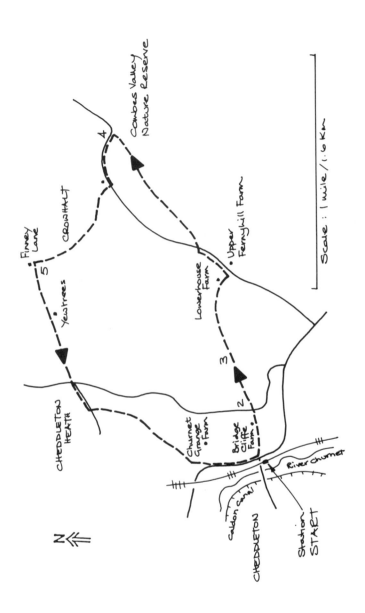

Combes Valley
Nature Reserve

CROWHALT

Finney
Lane

Yewtrees

Upper
Fernyhill Farm

Lowerhouse
Farm

CHEDDLETON
HEATH

Churnet
Grange
Farm

Bridge
Cliffe
Farm

River Churnet

Caldon Canal

CHEDDLETON

Station
START

Scale : 1 mile / 1.6 Km

N

path follows a dry-stone wall(with large pieces of stone) on the right up the hillside to cross a stile into the next field. Continue ahead and at the next boundary go through a gateway soon reaching the summit of Ferny Hill. Cross a double stile and head slightly right down the hill to go over another stile. Go to a stile by a gate and to a road. To the right is Coombes Valley Nature Reserve which is open to the public.

(4) Turn left here to return towards Cheddleton. Pass a farm on the right and then go over a wooden stile into an adjacent field. Keep ahead down the bank to cross another wooden stile. Then, bear slightly left across the next rough pasture. Cross a stile beneath a holly bush and turn right down the track. This curves right to cottages at Crowhalt but you turn left along a green track to a stile by a gate. Continue along this track for approximately 100 metres then cut right down the field to a stile by a tree in the bottom wall. Go through here and climb the bank up to a track before a barn at the historic farmstead at Finney Lane.

(5) Turn left and go through the gate to join a drive which passes by Yewtrees Farm to a crossroads at Cheddleton Heath. Cross over to Cheddleton Heath Road where nearby is another site of a cross similar to the one encountered earlier. Look for the signpost on the right which indicates the way to the left along a track. Go through a gate and pass by a bungalow and garden to a stile between hawthorn and holly. The path continues ahead and then heads slightly right to join an old track to the right of Churnet Grange Farm. Cross a stile here and keep ahead down the bank to the right of the farm in the direction of a stile in the bottom hedge with the caravan site on the opposite side of the road. Once on the road turn left back to the Railway Centre.

# 22. DENFORD

**Route:** Deep Hayes Country Park – Horse Bridge – Hazelhurst Locks – Hollinhurst Farm – Cats Edge – The Hollybush Inn – Deep Hayes Country Park

**Distance:** 3.5 miles

**Map:** O.S. Pathfinder 792 Kidsgrove and Leek

**Start:** Deep Hayes Country Park (Grid Reference: 962535)

**Access:** Those travelling by public transport should use the regular 218 bus (PMT weekdays),or Bakers on Sundays 223 to Longsdon. Walk half a mile to the Leek Branch of the canal.

*By Car* – Car travellers should follow the A53 towards Leek turning right for Deep Hayes as signposted.

## The Hollybush Inn (0538) 371819

The Hollybush borders the Caldon canal, its little porch leading into a cosy bar and to the right a lounge and conservatory. This friendly pub is always bustling with ramblers, boaters and locals popping in for a pint or a meal. It is also home to a well-known Tug of War team who refresh themselves after practising on a nearby ground. Sometimes, they can be heard as you walk by, a cacophony of grunting and groaning, sighs and relief!

The Hollybush Inn dispenses many cask-conditioned ales including Marstons Burton Bitter and Pedigree, Ansells Bitter and ABC, Ruddles Bitter and another guest beer which changes weekly. The Hollybush Inn is open until 4pm on Mondays to Fridays and then from 7pm in the evenings. It is open all day Saturday and usual Sunday hours. Food is served at lunchtimes until 3pm and all day Saturday. Families are welcome and there are seats outside. A good place to stop awhile before returning to Deep Hayes.

*The Hollybush*

## Deep Hayes

Deep Hayes Country Park has developed around a series of small reservoirs which are a haven for birds. The Park offers several short trails and there are waymarked walks farther afield.

# The Walk

(1) From the Visitor Centre retrace your steps to the entrance of the country park. Turn left and cross the bridge over the Caldon Canal and the railway line. Note the old station house, now a private dwelling, on the right. The road leads up to the Leek Branch of the Caldon Canal. Turn left onto the towpath before the bridge.

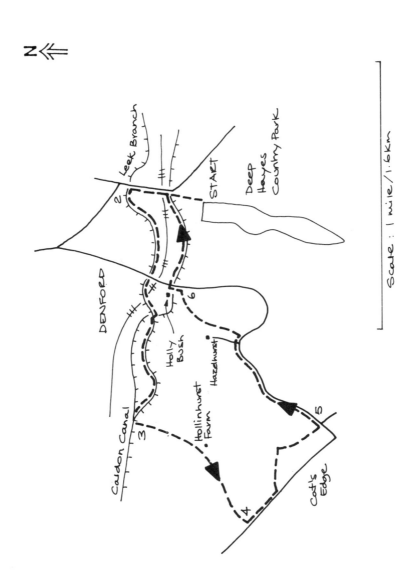

(2) Pass by cottages, go over the railway line and then cross the bridge before a cottage once over the aqueduct. The towpath soon reaches Hazelhurst locks where the Leek Branch joins the Caldon. This is a place to pause. The ornate footbridge dating from 1842, for example, is a masterpiece of canal architecture. However your way is before the canal at the locks. There is a stile on the right which leads up to a track. Once over bear left and cross the bridge and a stile (following the green waymarks).

(3) Climb away from the canals up a field. Go through the gateway. Then bear slightly right to head for a point to the right of a barn. There, you will find a stile by a water tank. Head slightly left across the next field to a stile by a holly bush opposite Hollinhurst Farm. Head towards an electricity pole where another stile is hidden by holly bushes. Once through the hedge keep slightly left through the next enclosure to another hidden stile and ahead again to a stone stile which sits to the left of a farm and barn. Walk straight on to pass to the left of a bungalow and towards two trees in the direction of the Victorian farmhouse. There are good views back over the Western Peak District from here.

(4) On the road go left and walk up the bank towards Cats Edge. At the top of the first steep section turn left along a track and as this bears left keep ahead through a gap-stile.

Continue ahead through the field to cross a stile by a water trough. This gets messy in Winter. Go ahead through a small enclosure to a stile which crosses a dry-stone wall. Turn right to walk along the Edge. Cross a small stone stile and keep ahead to a gateway with a farm to your right, then to another which leads onto a road at a junction.

(5) Turn left along the road signposted to Longsdon and Leek. This descends towards Denford, curving right by a farm and right again further down before dipping towards another cottage. Look for a drive on the left to Hazelhurst, by a stream. Just beyond is a gap-stile on the left. The path crosses a wooden stile by a gate and joins a track. The stream runs to the right. Walk down the track going through a gap-stile by a gateway. However, at the next one go right over a little bridge to cross a stile. Go straight on through a field to another stile by a barred gate. The Hollybush Inn is to your left, a temptation that is too good to miss.

(6) At the road go left and cross the canal bridge to turn left for the pub. Join the towpath and bear left to follow the canal back to Deep Hayes. The towpath passes on of the rare drawbridges on the Caldon and saunters beneath the branches of overhanging trees, a joy in all seasons but rather special when there has been a heavy frost. Go left up to the road and left for the entrance to Deep Hayes Country Park which is on the right.

# 23. LEEK

**Route:** Rushton Spencer – Heaton – Gun End – Back Hills Woods – Abbey Inn – Leek

**Distance:** 8 miles

**Map:** O.S. Leisure Map 24 – The White Peak

**Start:** The Royal Oak (Grid Reference: 938624)

**Access:** There is a regular bus service from the Potteries to Leek bus station, 5 minutes walk from the Market Square. Contact PMT for weekday service on (0782) 747000 or Bakers for Sunday service on (0782) 522101. This is a linear walk, the idea being to catch the bus to Rushton Spencer and walk back to Leek. There is a daily bus service 201 from Leek to Rushton operated by GM buses. Contact Staffordshire Bus for details on (0785) 223344. The route is known for its reliability.

## The Abbey Inn (0538) 382865

This handsome sandstone inn set in the hillside on the road to Meerbrook is delightful on a Summer's day when there are seats out on the patio surrounded by flowers in bloom. Built in 1702 possibly on the site of former such hostelries, it was here to serve travellers on the old Leek to Macclesfield Road which this ramble follows in part. Formerly called The Bowling Green the pub was renowned for its bowling (where the car park is today) but the change came in the 1950s. The name Abbey refers to nearby "Dieu la Cresse" abbey. There are still small remnants at Abbey Farm but this is private with no access.

The Abbey has one central bar which serves separate areas of the pub, a larger room to the left and a smaller one to the right. It is a friendly inn offering Draught Bass on hand-pull and a different guest beer each week so there's always a surprise in store. Food is on offer and finishing times are at 2pm lunchtimes and 8pm on Monday and Tuesday evening, 9pm on Wednesday to Saturday. The Abbey opens from 11am until 2.30pm at lunch on weekdays, 3pm on Saturdays and from 6.30pm in the evening.

Normal Sunday hours. Families are welcome and for those visiting the area, there is accommodation in an adjacent converted barn. This has a strong local following and walkers are made most welcome.

*The Earl Grey*

## More refreshments . . .

Leek is well-endowed with pubs of all shapes and sizes, including smaller traditional local pubs, such as The Earl Grey on Ashbourne Road or The Fountain in Fountain Street, both a few minutes walk away from Leek Bus station. Rushton Spencer has four pubs, two of which – The Knot and The Crown – are featured in Walk 30. There is also The Royal Oak (Burton-woods) and The Rushton Inn (Free House) on the main road. Afternoon tea is often available at Gun End Farm.

## Leek

The moorland town of Leek stands at the southern tip of the Pennines, a northern town by nature with its remaining mills, narrow streets and traditional town centre adding to its character. The town became famous for silk production as well as hosiery and dyeing. There are still chemical works by the Macclesfield Road. Leek attracts the farming community to market on Wednesdays when there are stalls in the Market Place. An excellent tourist information centre is situated here too. The town has many fine Victorian buildings designed or influenced by the famous Leek architect William Sugden including the fascinating Nicholson Institute with its lofty tower which can be seen for miles around.

# The Walk

(1) From The Royal Oak, turn left from the entrance and left again. Pass by a delightful row of stone built cottages and just before the school, take the first narrow lane on the right. This climbs up by houses and as it curves right to a house go left up to a stile by a wooden barred gate. The path leads up beneath a hollybush to a gap-stile and continues ahead with a fence and wall to the right. It cuts through a gap then runs along a little wedge of ground between the wooded slope and pasture. Cross a stile and walk along the hedge until it bears right. Your way is across the field towards a house where you exit just to the right of it onto a road.

(2) Turn left along the road and descend to a junction where you turn right to climb up to Heaton, an isolated hamlet nestled in this intriguing part of the moorlands. At the triangular junction turn left by a kiosk and then left again. Follow this for a short distance looking for a green lane off to the right, a lane which is shielded by bramble and nettles. It does improve but be forewarned that sections can get very wet.

(3) Follow this lovely old green lane up to Hawksley Farm. There is a good view of Tofthall on the right, a stone-built house of character standing forlorn across the fields. The track leads to a footbridge and passes between farm buildings and a bungalow. It continues ahead to the Wincle Road. Go left along it to pass a chapel. At the next sharp corner left, go right up a track by Gun End Farm which has a reputation for serving homemade cakes and afternoon teas.

(4) The track leaves the farmhouses behind and climbs up alongside a wood. The track and then green path follows the wall on the right and leads to a gap-stile which is crossed. There are good views from here back to the haunting outline of Shutlingsloe. Keep ahead until you reach a stile by a gate and onto a road. Keep ahead and as this bends right go left over a stile and sleeper bridge. There are old earthworks to the right and the path follows the fence straight on until another road is reached.

(5) Proceed ahead along the road as it climbs the shoulders of the sinister Gun Hill, a place known for its hangings in earlier centuries. One could not imagine a more dour place for a public execution to take place. As

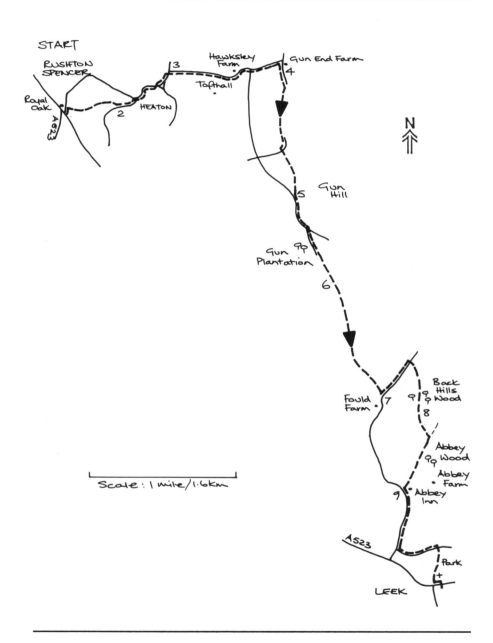

the road bears left by the car parking areas continue ahead along an aggregate track by a wind-break known as Gun Plantation. The gates are secured along here but at the end of the wood there is a stile leading into fields again, where there are views across to The Roaches and The Mermaid public house.

(6) A wall falls away to the right but you follow the traces of the sunken old road between Macclesfield and Leek. It drops down to a gap-stile and then continues along the route to a gap-stile in a dry-stone wall near a gate. The path continues to follow a line parallel to the old route, which is now tree lined. This descends to a stile beneath a large tree and down steps to the road just above Fould Farm.

(7) Turn left to climb the bank but before a house go right over a stile into a field. Walk straight down the bank to cross a tractor bridge and bear slightly right to a gate which leads into Back Hills Wood. The path is distinct for most parts of the year unless a littering of leaves obscures the way. It winds its way through the wood climbing to a stile in the top-right corner.

*The Abbey Inn*

(8) The path bears slightly right across the field to join another prominent section of the old road, again tree-lined. Walk ahead along a line parallel to the old road for the entire length of the field. Join a path which comes in from the left to bear right at the head of Abbey Wood. This well-used path proceeds ahead through stiles by gates. It then begins to descend the hillside through parkland above Abbey Farm, where the scant remains of Dieu-la-Cresse abbey have been maintained. It is, however, a private residence. The path heads for the Abbey Inn. Drop down to a stile and pass through the car park to the road.

(9) Turn left for Leek. Just before the Macclesfield Road, where Brindley's Mill is situated, turn left along Mill Road. This leads to a park where you turn right to walk up to St Edward's Church. Turn left for the Market Place.

# 24. MOW COP

**Route:** Mow Cop – The Bank – Scholar Green – Boarded Barn – Little Moreton Hall – Ackers Crossing – Mow Cop

**Distance:** 8 miles

**Map:** O.S. Pathfinder 792 Kidsgrove and Leek·

**Start:** The folly at Mow Cop (Grid Reference: 857574)

**Access:** There is a regular PMT bus to Mow Cop. Telephone (0782) 747000 for details.

*By Car* – Mow Cop can be approached from the A34 at Scholar Green or from Goldenhill off the A50 road. There is car parking near to the monument which is owned by the National Trust.

## The Cheshire View (0782) 514211

This old hillside pub was previously known as The Railway Inn despite being a long haul up from the site of the former station. Rail travellers would have been in need of refreshment by the time they had reached the hostelry. Its current name is most appropriate for the views from the lounge across Cheshire are spectacular. There is also a lively bar on the other side.

The Cheshire View serves a tasty pint of Banks's Mild, Marstons Burton Bitter and Pedigree and offers rolls at weekday lunchtimes and traditional lunch on Sundays. Families are welcome inside at lunch if eating but not in the evenings. There is an outdoor drinking area which is very popular in Summer. Opening times are from noon until 3pm and from 7pm in the evening Monday to Saturdays. Usual Sunday hours prevail.

*The Cheshire View, Mow Cop*

## Mow Cop

The hilltop quarrying settlement of Mow Cop became the scene of many mass meetings during the last century, gatherings which caused and popularised Primitive Methodism. The split from the Methodist church which was not to be healed for decades. Leaders such as Hugh Bourne would attract thousands of would-be worshippers to camp meetings on these hillsides and the followers were known locally as Ranters.

The folly at Mow Cop was one such location where people gathered. This mock castle was built in the 1750s to serve a completely different purpose. Nearby landowner, Randle Wilbraham thought the structure would improve the views from his home at Rode Hall. The sham castle is North Staffordshire's most noticeable monument for it can be seen for miles around. Now in National Trust ownership it is the starting point of the Mow Cop Trail (Staffordshire Way). This path threads through Staffordshire and is the subject of a companion book prepared by the authors. It is available in local bookshops.

*The Folly, Mow Cop*

# Little Moreton Hall

The famous architectural historian, Pevsner, described Little Moreton Hall as "happily reeling and somewhat disorderly". He was referring, of course, to the way in which parts of the house extrude and others lean at a considerable angle. It is certainly one of the finest half-timbered buildings in the land, surrounded by a moat and sheltering an inner cobbled courtyard. This fine building is also in the hands of the National Trust. Part of the house has been restored in recent years and a knot garden has been recreated for the pleasure of the visitor. Little Moreton Hall is to be found mid-way along the ramble.

*Little Moreton Hall*

# The Walk

(1) From the car park in front of the Mow Cop folly, turn left to pass by the junction with Top Station Road (which leads to the Cheshire View). Continue down High Street and by the old mill turn right to pass a shop and a small well in the wall, where an inscription reads:

*"Keep Thyself Pure*
*The Parsons Well, 1857"*

At the junction cross to a gap-stile by the Primitive Methodist Chapel dating from 1860. This was built on the site of a former chapel of smaller proportions.

(2) The path descends at the back of gardens, unfortunately fouled by dogs in places so tread gingerly. The final section drops down steps to a track. Go left and walk to a junction before a bungalow. Go right here down what must have been an old trackway from the quarries down the hillside. Cross a stile and keep ahead to join a made-up track known as The Brake. At the road turn left.

(3) Walk by houses and at the corner cross the road opposite Mow Cop Village Hall. Go over the stile on the left and follow the track which bears right with a hedge to the right. This leads to a junction of tracks. Walk straight on, passing a stile on the left and right, into the field ahead. Turn left to follow the wire fencing on the left until it curves right. Go left over a stile here (signposted) and now follow the hedge to your left. This brings you to a footbridge over a stream and you then walk between electricity poles and fencing. Head slightly left to a stile which comprises all manner of scrap and proceed ahead through two small enclosures by way of wooden stiles onto a drive.

(4) This leads shortly to a road but just before the junction go right over a stile into a large field. The path is signposted. Bear slightly right across a field. There is no real landmark but look for a footbridge over a small stream. Once over keep ahead but ease closer towards the tree lined brook to cross a stile. You cross another stile by a barred gate into woodland and old workings. Follow the main track but avoid a path deviating right. Notice a stile introducing a path coming in from the right and now look for a path on the left which leads up a stile and field.

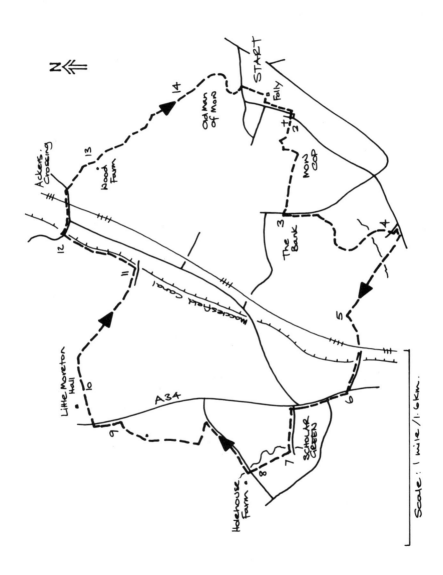

(5) Head slightly right across the field to the far corner where you go over a stile beneath a tree. Keep company with the hedge to your right which brings you to an under-bridge. Go over a track and continue ahead over the canal bridge. There is a choice of routes here. If you want a shorter ramble, bear right down to the canal towpath and then left along it. Others should go left and the little path winds right to join a cul de sac. This leads down to the main Congleton Road in Scholar Green.

(6) Turn right to follow the pavement by shops on the right and Church Lane on the left. Cross the road at some stage along here. Opposite the next main junction, Station Road, turn left down a lane, signposted as a footpath. The road becomes a green track, passes the gardens of two dwellings and narrows to a footbridge.

(7) Go over this and walk for no more than a hundred paces to find a stile on the right. Cross this and walk ahead with a wire fence to your left and a hedge soon on the right. At the end of the hedge the path curves slightly right to dip towards the stream and then cuts right to a stile by the little red brick bridge.

(8) Cross the stile, which is less than stable, then turn right to walk over the bridge. You might catch a glimpse to the left of the pretty church at Odd Rode beyond Holehouse farm. Follow the quiet metalled road towards the main A34 Congleton road but as the lane rises bear left through a gate. The path follows the hedge down to an indent in the field. Cross the stile here and continue along the left-hand side of the hedge. This comes to a gateway. Go through it and walk towards the farm building. The path proceeds through another gate and at the corner cuts right through rough and often muddy ground to another gate. Continue ahead along the field's edge and around to a stile. Go right over it and walk to a hedge where a stile exits onto the main A34 road.

(9) Walk on the pavement until the turning for Moreton Hall is reached, the splendid outline of the historic building standing behind tall trees. The hall is open to the public and light lunches and home-made teas are also available to those visiting. Cross the road with extreme caution and walk by the car park. The path continues by a wooden hut, along the drive in front of the hall and crosses a stile to the right of an entrance to a private farm.

(10) Once over the stile walk straight on to cross another stile and head very slightly right to another stile by a gate. There are excellent views of Mow Cop from here. The path now follows the field boundary on the left ahead, then cuts left over a stile and onwards to cross another by a gate. Most of these stiles are marked with the initials "SCW", referring to the South Cheshire Way, a route devised by The Mid-Cheshire Footpath Society from Grindley Brook near Whitchurch to Mow Cop, linking The Sandstone Trail to the Staffordshire Way.

(11) The path leads to a stile just to the right of the canal bridge over the Macclesfield canal, a testimony to the engineering skills of two great canal engineers, Brindley and Telford. Cross the stile and turn left on the towpath to go under the bridge. The handsome red brick building on the right is Ramsdell Hall. Follow this until the settlement of Ackers Green where you proceed under the next bridge before going left to climb steps up to the road.

(12) Turn left and pass by houses. At the corner turn left again along a road to Ackers Crossing. Cross the tracks with care as the trains thunder along this section. Walk along the metalled road but as it bears left you continue ahead along the track which begins to climb the hillside. Pass by Wood Farm on your right and not far beyond look for a green track on the right rising up to a gateway into a pasture.

(13) Head across the field to the right of the chimney stack landmark. The farmhouse soon comes into view. The path skirts the right of the garden and then climbs more steeply alongside an old track and near to the wood. It eventually sweeps left to a gap in the top left corner to enter the wood. The path now bears left for about 20 paces and then turns right to pass between holly bushes through a muddy section. It climbs remorselessly upwards to a small wooden gap-stile exiting into a field.

(14) Walk onwards through two fields to a stile which leads into rougher ground. The path proceeds to a track. Turn right to pass by a cottage and to The Old Man of Mow, a mysterious outline of rock left by quarrying in earlier times, the shape said to resemble the face of an old man. The track passes between houses and cottages to Castle Road. Cross it and walk through rough ground back to Mow Cop folly.

# 25. BIDDULPH

**Route:** Biddulph Country Park – Biddulph Park – The Talbot Inn – Fold Lane – Biddulph Country Park

**Distance :** 3 miles

**Map:** O.S. Pathfinders 792 Kidsgrove and Leek and 776 Congleton

**Start:** Biddulph Grange Country Park (Grid Reference: 894594)

**Access:** Biddulph Grange and adjacent country park are served on a Mondays to Saturdays by Bakers Coaches from Hanley (Tel: 0782 522101) Biddulph town centre, one mile away, is also served regularly by PMT, including a Sunday service.

*By Car* – Biddulph Grange Country Park is signposted from the A527 road from The Potteries to Congleton. There is ample car parking.

## The Talbot (0782) 512608

The Talbot is a fine old stone-built pub, a few minutes' walk from Biddulph Grange Country Park. There is a traditional front bar, and lounge rooms to the left and rear in this welcoming inn. The Talbot offers the acclaimed Highgate Mild, a creamy brown brew from the Highgate brewery in Walsall, and Draught Bass. The Talbot is open all day on Mondays to Fridays and for most of Saturday except from 4pm to 6.30pm. Usual Sunday hours. Food is available until 2.30pm at lunchtimes and Friday to Sunday evenings until 10pm. The Talbot welcomes families and there is an outside patio area with tables, which is popular during the summer months.

## Biddulph

The small North Staffordshire town of Biddulph gives way to higher moorland ground rising to Lask and Congleton Edges. The town centre is a mile distance from the old quarter centred around Biddulph Church on the Congleton Road.

Just behind lies the recently re-opened Victorian gardens At Biddulph Grange. These were created over a twenty-year period from 1840 by the Bateman family and their friend Edward Cooke. The house and gardens were sold to major industrialist Robert Heath in the early 1870s and he enhanced the gardens and house during the latter years of the last century. In 1923 the house and gardens were purchased by the Health Authority and for the better part of its existence was an orthopaedic hospital. In the late 1980s Staffordshire Moorlands District Council and other bodies sought to find a way to restore these magnificent gardens. The National Trust is now in the process of rejuvenating this exceptional horticultural work of art. It is open to the public throughout the Summer but closes in the harshest Winter months.

Next door is Biddulph Grange Country Park, which takes in some of the former Grange grounds. The park offers several short circular walks through mainly deciduous woodland leading up to Hurst, a name which reflects an Anglo Saxon origin where woodland has been cleared for cultivation.

*The Talbot, Biddulph*

# The Walk

(1) The walk commences at the Visitor centre, Biddulph Grange Country Park, where there are toilets and picnic tables as well as an exhibition area. Turn left from the entrance to walk up a well laid out path alongside the cascading brook. At the upper reach take the right fork to climb up to Hurst Road. Go right and walk along the road to the ornate Spring House with its turrets and high walls.

(2) At the far end of the house as the road bends right keep ahead up a "No Through Road" as signposted. This bends left and gives a wonderful view of Biddulph Moor and the outcrops characteristic of this area. The view also opens up to Mow Cop and down the valley to Congleton. Go left opposite an entrance to a house to enter fields.

(3) Walk ahead to a gateway with large rocks making up the boundary. The path follows a green track with a farm to the left and Hurst Quarry beyond. Proceed through another gap into rougher ground beneath an edge. The path rises gently away from the left fence. There is a small enclosure and remains of a building to the left. At the corner go over a stile on the left. Then, bear right to cross a field to a road. Turn left along the road which soon passes Aladdins Cave, a tumble of surplus stock and other goods on sale to the public.

(4) Follow the lane and, as it begins to descend by a wood, go left opposite houses at a road junction along a farm access track leading into the wood, where often a woodpecker can be heard. At the corner, go right down a woodland track. Cross a path and continue down to a drive. Keep ahead with a hall to the left. Bear slightly left beneath the chestnut trees and across parkland. There is a view here of an ogee turret belonging to the ruined Biddulph Old Hall, said to have been built for Francis Biddulph in the late 16th century and partly destroyed in the English Civil War. The ruins stand near to a farm and both are on private property. The path leads to a track which continues to a road.

(5) Turn right and at the corner left for the Talbot Inn. Before, however, are steps down to an old mill pool, now home to ducks and coots. The path follows a drive to the left of the house and by a wooden garage to become a woodland path. It soon comes to a small stone bridge with a

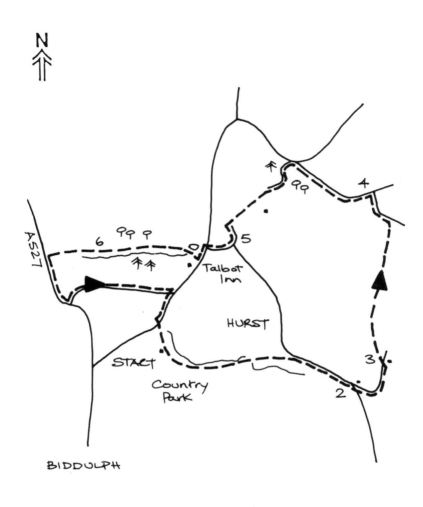

Scale : 1 mile / 1.6 km

path underneath leading into the clough. This was the Box Avenue from Biddulph Old Hall into this watery glen.

(6) There is a stile ahead. Cross this and follow the field's edge down the hillside, over a stile, to a footbridge. Exit onto a pavement by the main road and go left. Turn left again up Fold Lane to a junction by the Post Office and then bear right to return to the country park.

*Old Mill Pool, Biddulph*

# 26. RUDYARD

**Route:** Rudyard railway station – Longsdon Grange – Lyme House – Blake Meadows – Gratton – Horton – Rudyard

**Distance:** 5 miles

**Map:** O.S. Outdoor Leisure 24 – The White Peak

**Start:** The old Rudyard railway station car park (Grid Reference: 955579)

**Access:** Unfortunately, the bus service is very limited to Rudyard. Telephone Staffordshire Busline for details on (0785) 223344

*By Car* – Turn right off the A523 Leek to Macclesfield road at Poolend. The car park is signposted before the village but take care as the turning is a sharp left turn after the railway bridge.

## The Crown ( 0538) 33275

The Crown is a gem of a pub to be found down a no-through road just beyond the church in Hofton. This friendly hostelry with an open fire in the large fireplace by the bar in winter months offers Marstons Pedigree on hand-pull. There is also a larger seating area away from the bar and a games room. The Crown serves food at lunchtimes until 2pm except Monday. Opening times are from noon until 3pm and from 7pm in the evening on Mondays to Saturdays. Usual Sunday hours prevail.

## Rudyard

Rudyard has been a retreat for those living in the Potteries for well over a hundred years, a destination which was opened up by the North Staffordshire Railway. The lake happens to be a large reservoir built to the design of the genius James Brindley in the 1790s as a water supply for the Caldon and Trent and Mersey Canals. What a magnificent feat of engineering it is. The village of Rudyard has changed little since the turn of the century except for new housing in recent years. Nor has the nearby hamlet of Horton with its medieval church where a cross was

*Miniature Railway, Rudyard*

erected as a memorial to a young Moorland poet, George Heath who died at an early age. Nearby stands the handsome red brick vicarage and down the road the forlorn Horton Hall, described by Pevsner as a reflection of the Cotswolds rather than the Moorlands.

# The Walk

(1) Return to the road from the car park at Rudyard Old Station and turn left to pass by a garage on the right. Bear left along the feeder canal which soon reaches a nature reserve beneath Harracles Mill. On the hillside to the right is Harracles Hall, once home to the Wedgwood family (of Josiah Wedgwood fame). The feeder bears left and soon sweeps right under Longsdon Edge. Continue until you reach an ornate tractor bridge over the feeder and Cowhay Wood and nature reserve ahead. Do not proceed but instead go right over a bridge and climb up the steep bank with a wall to the left.

(2) The view over to Leek and the Peak District improves as you gain height. Go through a gap stone stile and walk ahead to another by a gate. Once through, turn left and follow a dry-stone wall but before the end of the field turn right up the bank to cross yet another stile by a gate. Go straight on to the summit, through a narrow enclosure to a gap-stile by a gate. To the right, views to Rudyard Lake and Bosley

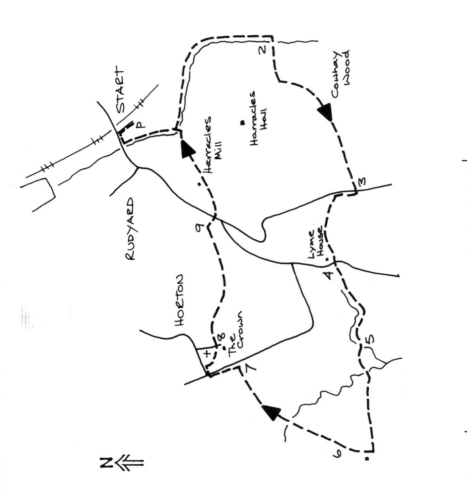

Minn open up. Walk straight on to a gap-stile by gate and then slightly left in the next field with a farm to the left and one on the right. Simply keep ahead through gap-stiles until the path reaches a road.

(3) Turn right and pass by a house and farm on the left. There is a perfectly reasonable path here but it is very cluttered at Lyme House. If you prefer, you can stay on the road and turn left at the junction to walk back to Lyme House. Those who are seeking a challenge should follow the instructions as follows. Go through a gate on the left as signposted and follow the field edge on the right down to a stile. Cross it and then at the next boundary a double stile. The turn left along a track. You cross another stile by a gate and continue to another gateway on the left (rather then bearing right into a field). This track drops down to the rear of Lyme House. The path does not seem clear here, for there are several implements and pieces of machinery to encounter. Come to the back of barns. Your way is ahead to the left of the buildings to pass by trailers et al to a barred gate. Cross the stream to exit through a gap-stile onto the road by the signpost, looking back at the less-than-comforting sign "Stay In Your Vehicle . . . Dogs Loose".

(4) Cross the road and there is a stile on the right of a gateway leading into rough pasture. The paths are less distinct throughout the next section but clear nevertheless. Go straight ahead to cross a stream and then follow it down the field and through an old gateway to another gateway. Continue alongside the stream. The path bends right as the stream runs underneath the hedge on your right.

(5) At the end of this hedge cross a stile beneath a tree and cross the stream. Go left along the far bank of the stream, a place where herons like to linger. As it bears left, cut across the field to a hawthorn hedge. Cross here and walk to the left of the house where a stile is crossed. Go slightly left to cross a footbridge (in a poor state) and head in a similar direction to the corner. Go straight on through a gap-stile and ahead to two metal rods making a gap in a hedge. You enter a larger field where your way is slightly right up the hillside walking almost up to the farm house but just before going right through a gap-stile by a water trough.

(6) Walk ahead to the next gap-stile and then head slightly right down the field in the direction of an electricity pylon. Cross a gap-stile and proceed in a similar direction across fields to a stone slab footbridge, the

landmark being Horton Church in the near distance. The path bears left following a hedge on your right up the bank. This leads to a gateway and stile. Continue up the bank towards a house and a road.

(7) Turn left and at the junction by Horton Hall go right. Bear right by the telephone kiosk opposite the hall and follow the path as it meanders across a small enclosure to the churchyard. The path passes by cottages to the right of the churchyard and down steps. Turn right for The Crown.

*The Crown*

(8) Having refreshed yourself go right through a stile opposite the pub car park before reaching the churchyard again. The path drops down the hillside quite steeply and then curves right through a gap. It heads gently left in the next field to cross a stile, continues ahead at first then bends left to cross another stile. The views across to the Roaches are good from this vantage point. There is a farm in the valley to the right and the well-worn path heads in the direction of a little loop of road, leaving the field by a stile.

(9) Go right and cross the road to turn left by a house with an old conservatory. Walk along the drive towards Harracles mill, now a private residence. As the drive nears the buildings, go through a stile on the right into fields and proceed with the hedge to your left. Cross a stile beneath a tree and go straight on again. Cross a stile onto the feeder canal and turn left. At the road bear right to return to the car park.

*Lych-gate at Horton Church*

# 27. HULME END

**Route:** Hulme End – Brund Mill – Sheen – Townend – Hulme End

**Distance:** 3 miles

**Map:** O.S. Outdoor Leisure 24 The Peak District – White Peak

**Start:** Car Park, Hulme End (Grid Reference:. 106594)

**Access:** Hulme End is served by buses daily from Buxton. There is also a direct link from Hanley on Saturdays which is ideal for exploring this part of the Moorlands. Contact Staffordshire Busline on (0785) 223344 for details.

*By Car* – Travel on the A52 to Froghall, then the B5053 to Warslow. Take the right turn (B5054) to Hulme End.

## The Manifold Valley Hotel (0298) 84537

This imposing mellow stoned hotel at the road junction to Alstonefield was built originally to serve the terminus of the Manifold Light Railway. Its earlier name, The Light Railway, used to reflect this. The hotel retains a popularity in the area with walkers, campers and cyclists seeking its well kept beers and good food. There is a bustling bar to the left of the entrance and a dining room to the right. It also has en suite accommodation. The Manifold Valley Hotel is open from noon until 2.30pm at lunch and from 7pm in the evenings on Mondays to Saturdays. Usual Sunday hours prevail. Food is available at lunch until 2pm and until 9pm in the evening. The beers include Wards Sheffield Bitter, Darley Thorne Mild and Best Bitter and guest beers on Summer weekends.

Families are welcome but please note that there are no facilities inside for families who are not eating. There are, however, seats outside where you can sit back and watch the cyclists go by.

*Manifold Valley Hotel*

## Hulme End

The Moorlands village of Hulme End was once the northern-most terminal of the Manifold Valley Light Railway, a narrow gauge (2ft 6 in) extension of the North Staffordshire Railway from Waterhouses. Passengers wishing to visit Hartington were expected to travel by carriage or on foot for the remainder of the journey. Some railway buildings belonging to this remarkable little railway still stand, despite its closure in the 1930s. They stand to the left of the car park. Every year, a miniature railway service is operated from here (on four weekends in June to early July) part-way down the valley, the proceeds being donated to charity. The engine, which has been modelled on the earlier light railway stock, is engineered by a local industrialist with an interest in steam traction. The track-bed is now for the most part a linear walking and cycle route passing through the exceptional scenery of the Manifold with Thors Cave and Wetton Mill attracting thousands every year. Hulme End is often the turn around point for those spending a day in the Manifold and has a camp site and village shop as well the hotel.

*The village stores, Hulme End*

Sheen is much quieter (although Hulme End could not be described as crowded), a small village nestled around the Victorian church of St Luke on higher ground. It is a farming community and has over the years sported a famous Sheen Farmers Tug-of-War team competing in world competitions.

# The Walk

(1) From the car park off the B5054 road to Warslow, turn right towards the village but at the corner by an old chapel turn left. Walk out of the village and after the bend look for a stile on the right. Go slightly left to a stone stile. Proceed along the field's edge to go through a gate with a farm standing across the field to the left. At the end of the pasture go through a stone stile.  Go ahead through a large field, with a view to Sheen church on the right. Cross a stile by a junction of hedges and you now need to cross to the other side of the hedge but still proceeding to a

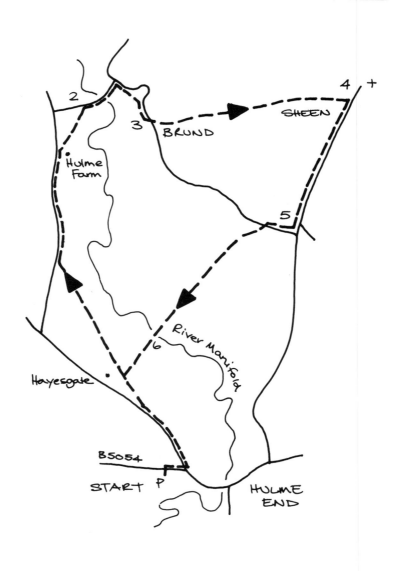

field corner. Cross a stile onto the road. Go right along the lane to a point just beyond Hulme Farm. Cross a stile on the right and head diagonally across the field to exit by a stile next to a gate.

(2) Turn right along the lane and cross the Manifold near an old mill. Climb the bank to the junction and look to see if afternoon tea is being served on the left by the junction. Go right just before the junction along a little used path which crosses a stream and climbs a hill, heading slightly right through a gap in the wire fence to a footpath sign and step stile leading back onto the road. Go right to continue through the quiet hamlet of Brund, where old buildings stand in the shade of the trees giving a feeling of timelessness.

(3) Opposite a farmhouse, go left up a narrow track which soon widens. Go through a gap into a field and ahead through a gap-stile as the track proceeds, now without a hedge. The old gatestones look reminiscent of Robin Hood's Picking Rods near Glossop, but they are genuinely remains of fine gateposts or gap-stiles rather than mysterious guide stones. The old stiles do act as markers though for your path leaves the old track to bear slightly left. Go through another stile with a ruined barn to the left and follow the farmer's "lollipop" style marker posts through the next field to a gap-stile by a gate and left of a barn. Head slightly left onto the road.

(4) In Sheen, the church is to the left. Unless visiting, turn right to pass the village pub, The Staffordshire Knot, and at the end of the village come to a staggered junction where a tree stands:

"This tree was planted March 10th 1883 by the incumbent and parishioners of Sheen in honour of the marriage of Albert Prince of Wales and Alexandra Princess of Denmark."

It is interesting for its size, given over 100 years of growth.

(5) Go right at the junction to walk by an engineering works which includes a miniature railway in the grounds. As you descend turn left along a track at the rear of the works. Go through a gap-stile by a gate and ahead to pass through another. Continue ahead where the track bears left to the sheltered buildings at Low End,ie keeping to the left of the wall down the field. There is a building across the field to the right.

Cross the stile in the field corner and proceed onwards with a hedge to the left at first but bearing slightly right to a footbridge over the babbling waters of the Manifold.

(6) Once over, continue straight on to a beautiful large stone gap-stile, complete with old milk churn. The path now climbs the bank and heads towards the roof of a farm at Hayesgate. The stile stands to the left of the water trough. Cross it and go left here to retrace your steps back to Hulme End.

# 28. ROYAL COTTAGE

**Route:** Royal Cottage – Gib Tor – Lower Stake Gutter (cut off point) – Blue Hills – Dains Mills – Upper Hulme

**Distance:** 2.5 miles circular, 4 miles linear

**Map:** O.S. Outdoor Leisure 24 – The White Peak

**Start:** The Royal Cottage (Grid Reference: 026641)

**Access:** This is a linear walk with a circular cut-off option. Those travelling by bus will find a daily PMT X23 bus between Leek Upper Hulme and Royal Cottage (Tel: 0782 747000). There is also a Baker's Coaches 223 "Moorland Rider" on Sundays (Tel: 0782 522101) and a regular bus link from Tittesworth Reservoir to Upper Hulme on Summer Sundays.

*By Car* – Car users might like to park near The Rock public house at Upper Hulme (just off the A53 Leek to Buxton Road) and catch the bus for a short hop up to Royal Cottage. There is a cut-off point allowing a circular walk from Royal Cottage too. There is very limited parking off the main road near The Royal Cottage and Winking Man public houses.

## Ye Olde Rock Inn (0538) 300324

Ye Olde Rock Inn stands beneath the brooding masses of The Roaches and Ramshaw Rocks, a 17th century hostelry (now Grade II listed building) which has served many a traveller on this high level road between Leek and Buxton. It is a spacious pub and in 1988 a new Hikers and Climbers bar was built to welcome the walker from the moors. Boots are allowed in this part of the pub which is tiled. The entrance is to the rear. A ladies toilet in the family room is used by ladies wearing boots. This special provision means that the carpeted lounge areas are not for those wearing boots! Draught Bass is on sale.

Ye Olde Rock Inn is open from 7pm every evening (i.e. no lunchtime opening) and from noon until 2.30pm at weekends. Food orders finish at

2pm Saturday lunch, 1.45pm Sunday lunch, 9.30 Monday evening and 10pm on other evenings. The landlord mentions that walkers are very welcome here but please remember that as with most country inns nowadays eating your own food is not permitted. Families are also specially catered for with the provision of a Family Room and there are seats outside.

*Ye Olde Rock*

## Upper Hulme

This moorland village has grown up around the fast running waters draining the Roaches, allowing the development of a few small mils, some of which survive but not in working order. The Roaches have become extremely popular during the past decade, so much so that the Peak Park is concerned about the congestion caused by car parking on roads in the area not meant for such volumes of leisure traffic. If you have been walking along the edges recently, you might note that the paths are becoming eroded and climbers seem to be hanging on every crag. This is understandable. This dramatic scenery makes for compelling walking and is a dream for the climber. There is a case for restraint and the route chosen here is one of the quieter routes not heavily walked.

*The Roaches from Tittesworth*

# The Walk

(1) The Winking Man is probably the best known landmark on the A53 route but just beyond the turning to Longnor on the right is a little known public house known as The Royal Cottage. From here turn next left and follow the road as it descends by a coniferous plantation to a house on the right, Gibb Tor.

(2) Before a stream turn left. The path leads left into woodland, climbs then dips as it winds alongside a wire fence and small wall. It emerges onto moorland through a gap-stile, with impressive rock shapes ahead

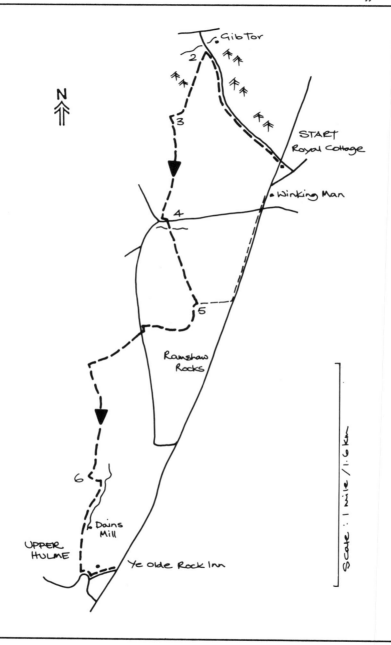

N

Gib Tor

2

3

START
Royal Cottage

Winking Man

4

5

Ramshaw
Rocks

6

Dains
Mill

UPPER
HULME

Ye Olde Rock Inn

Scale : 1 mile / 1.6 km

beckoning you across the wet ground. The well-worn path heads to a point above a ground water tank, winding around the heads of streams. It then cuts right to pass through a gap by a stone outcrop and bears left through a gap-stile to climb up to a higher outcrop.

(3) Follow the wall along the ridge then crosses before a stile at another outcrop. Pass to the left and beneath the rocks and descend to a road by a cottage known as The Cornerhouse. Go left at the junction and then turn right over a stile towards Ramshaw Rocks.

(4) Walk ahead towards a fence, across a stream and then left along the fencing to the corner and then right along the fence to a corner. Cross a stile and go straight on through moorland at first but then winding up the hillside in the direction of Ramshaw Rocks. The path narrows and steepens as it climbs through heather and bilberry to meet a dry-stone wall on the left and then a sunken track. Those seeking a cut off point should turn left here to return to the main road. It is a quarter of a mile walk on the road back to The Winking Man, although there is a fairly-wide verge on the facing side.

(5) Otherwise turn right to follow the track, which becomes a path, down, as it bears left and then right through the heather to a road by a smallholding. Turn left but almost immediately right over a stile. Head slightly left to join a dry-stone wall down the hillside to a stile. Cross it and continue ahead. The fence bears left but you walk slightly right through old workings towards a stream in a small clough on the right. Look for the footbridge on the right where you join a well-walked path. Go left along the narrow path which winds through gorse and through an old stone gap-stile. The path descends to a stile, then dips to another before crossing the stream. Climb up to another stile and cross it. Proceed ahead now (to the left of the electricity pole) to cross a stile in a fence. Bear right alongside the wall but head head slightly left across the field towards the protuding corner of a dry-stone wall. Cross a stile by a barred gate and follow the tractor track between two electricity poles. There's a farm to the left across the valley. Hen Cloud stands majestically before you. The tractor track drops down to another track.

(6) Turn left and as the track bears left go ahead over a stile by a barred gateway through rough ground. Then right to follow a well-used path down the valley to the ruins of Dains Mill. It then meets a lane which is

followed into Upper Hulme where two left turns are made for Ye Old Rock Inn.

*Outcrop near Ramshaw Rocks*

# 29. LONGNOR

**Route:** Longnor – Fawfieldhead – Boosley Grange – Reapsmoor – Manifold Valley – Longnor

**Distance:** 6 miles

**Map:** O.S. Outdoor Leisure 24 The Peak District – White Peak Area

**Start:** The Square, Longnor (Grid Reference: 088648)

**Access:** Longnor is served by buses from Buxton daily and there is a Saturdays only link from Hanley which proves ideal for this ramble. Contact (0785) 223344 for details.

*By Car* – Take the A53 to Buxton, turning right just after The Winking Man public house. There is parking in The Square at Longnor.

## The Butchers Arms, Reapsmoor (0298) 84477

The Butchers Arms is a survivor from the days when farming and running a pub was far more commonplace. Reapsmoor is an isolated community and this hostelry is a popular venue for the farms and cottages hereabouts. It does, however, have a warm welcome for the rambler too, often with a roaring fire in winter. The pub is split into several areas and Marston's Pedigree and a guest beer are usually on hand-pull.

The Butchers Arms is open at lunchtimes from noon until 3pm except Mondays and from 7pm in the evenings. Usual Sunday hours prevail. Food is served at lunch and evenings from 7pm until 10pm but not Wednesday evenings. By the way, the hosts do not object to ramblers bringing their own sandwiches. Altogether a welcoming pub for the walker.

*The Butcher's Arms, Reapsmoor*

## Longnor

Longnor is a large village or small town in the northernmost point of Staffordshire depending on how you define the term township. It would have been important in previous centuries as a market place where fairs and gatherings were held. The Market Hall, now a craft centre, gives the Square a characterful feeling standing on opposite the Crewe and Harper Arms. A little alleyway leads off to a restaurant and a thread of lanes bring you to the imposing church which dates from Norman times although is mostly of Georgian restoration. Longnor has several welcoming pubs around the Square so the walker will not go thirsty in these parts.

# The Walk

(1) From The Square follow the road to Royal Cottage and Leek, passing

*Resting at Longnor*

the Horseshoes Inn. There are unusual views of the Upper Dove from here, across to Chrome and Parkhouse. The road dips down to cross The Manifold at Longnor Bridge and then climbs up by the old saw mills to Heath House Farm on the left. Pass the farmhouse and then turn left along an access road to barns belonging to the farm. At the corner of the large barn go right along a concrete road to the end of the building and turn left to the rear of the barn.

(2) Leave the farm buildings to drop down to a hollow and climb up through gorse to a stone step stile(signpost here). Cross this and head slightly left up the bank almost parallel with a gully on your right. The view back to Longnor makes the climb worthwhile. Look for a lone signpost in the wall ahead where a gap-stile is found. Once through keep ahead to a barred gate which exits onto a road. Go left and walk to a scattering of houses at Fawfieldhead.

(3) Turn right at the junction and, before Sycamore Farm, go left by a line of sycamore trees, through a gap-stile. Walk down the bank between two more trees and then turn right to follow the hedge below the farm to a little bridge. Once over, bear slightly left up the bank and across the field to a wooden stile and gap-stile. Cross both and follow the path as it heads slightly left to a follow a wire fence. Cross a stile by a gate and head towards Hallhill Farm. Go over a stile beneath a holly bush, then keep ahead to a footpath sign to the right of the farmhouse.

(4) Cross the stile and walk by buildings, over the drive and ahead to cross a stile, despite the zealous dogs. Proceed ahead down the bank to a wooden gap-stile by an electricity pole. Cross it and continue in the same direction through pleasant moorland farming country. Join a remnant of a hedge and go through a gateway, keeping close to the hedge on the right. Boosley Grange Farm is the landmark.

(5) Cross a stile and footbridge. The path then curves to the right before climbing the bank up to a finger post before the barn. Turn left and walk to the end of the buildings where another signpost directs you to the right to cross a stile in fencing, then to another. Bear slightly right in the next field to cross a stream, one of the many small brooks draining the moors into the Manifold. Go through a gap-stile. Cross a track and continue ahead, down to a stile by a gate.

(6) Follow the hedge for 100 metres until it curves right and then cut off

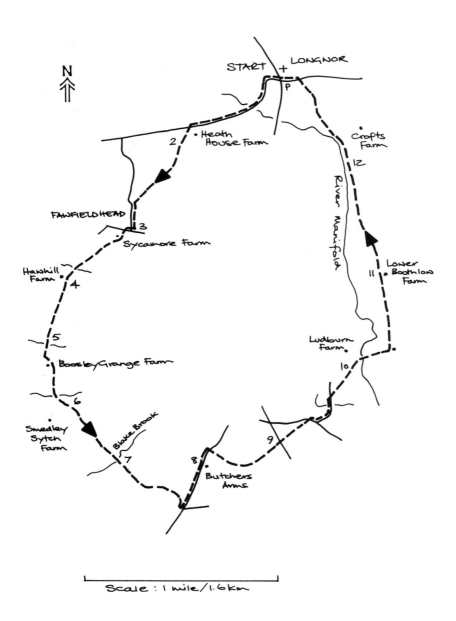

Scale : 1 mile/1.6 km

left to the remains of a hawthorn hedge as Smedley Sytch Farm is seen on the right. Follow it to a gate where a stile can be found to the right. Once over continue ahead to another gate where the stile is to the left. Cross it and walk through rough ground to a footbridge (or you can ford Blake Brook at this point).

(7) Keep ahead to cross a stile by a gate. A track runs to the right of the wall but the path keeps to the left side. Cross a gap-stile and continue ahead through an enclosure where there are two barns. Go left at the end to follow the field's edge. Go through a gap-stile and straight on to another. The path runs in the same direction until the next field where it curves right towards a farmhouse on the right. To the left of the building look for a stile which allows a cut through at the corner of the garden to the road. Turn left for The Butchers Arms.

(8) Turn left from the entrance of The Butchers Arms and follow the road as it curves to the right. Cross a stile (signposted) into a field and walk ahead through gap-stiles, then over a small wooden footbridge. Go straight on to another gap-stile with a footbridge either side. Once over these go ahead to cross two narrow enclosures by way of gap-stiles. Head slightly right aiming for a gateway, then onward to the narrowest of gap-stiles. Keep ahead at the junction of tracks, despite there being stiles on the left and right. The track is festooned with tormentil, vetch, heather and gorse. It leads down to a road.

(9) Cross the road and go through a gap-stile. Walk down the field to another gap-stile and continue ahead to a stile leading onto a road by a farm. Walk ahead to a junction where you turn left. The road bends left to cross a stream. Go right over a stile into a field (signposted) the head slightly left to a wooden stile. Cross it and turn right. Follow the hedge on your right and just beyond the corner cross a stile. Follow the hedge and stream ahead until you reach a track to the right of a gate. The building to your left is Ludburn Farm.

(10) Go left and at the corner go right over a footbridge to cross the infant Manifold. Continue ahead to a gap-stile and up a green lane to a farm. Go left just before over a stone step stile and ahead to a gateway. The return section follows a well-walked path through the Manifold Valley to Longnor which can now be seen again. Go through gap-stiles to a barn. The way is just to the right of it, to a double stile guarding a

sleeper footbridge. Proceed now towards the right-hand field boundary and Lower Boothlow Farm.

(11) Go through the gate by the farm onto a track. Go over a gap-stile and continue ahead with trees to your right. Cross a double stile and bridge and in the next field the path heads left towards the river, crossing a gap and wooden stile into a larger water meadow. Over Boothlow Farm is to your right. Follow the path as it eases closer to the Manifold. The river curves left at a point where Crofts Farm can be seen on the right, surrounded by a dozen or more narrow enclosures.

(12) The path reaches another larger field and curves right to go through a stile in a dry-stone wall (With a Single File Notice). Head slightly left up to a barn. The path curves to a stone step-stile in the top corner. It then heads for the far right-hand corner of the immediate barn. Cross the step stile to the right of the gate into the farmyard. Turn right to walk up the drive to a junction. Turn left for the Square.

*The craft centre in the Square at Longnor*

# 30. RUSHTON SPENCER

**Route:** Rushton – Rushton Church – Oulton – Woodhouse Green – Dane Valley – Rushton

**Distance:** 3 miles

**Map:** O.S. Pathfinder Map 776, Congleton

**Start:** The Knot Inn, Rushton Spencer (Grid Reference: 937625)

**Access:** Rushton is on the 201 bus link between Derby and Manchester offering a daily service.

*By Car* – travel on the A523. Turn off for the Knot Inn in Rushton and then left after the pub for a small car park on the Staffordshire Way.

## The Knot Inn, Rushton Spencer (0260 )226238

The Knot Inn stands opposite the old Rushton Spencer railway station on Station Road. The pub retains a bar and has a larger lounge cum dining room to the rear. This deservedly popular house serves Boddingtons and Theakstons Bitter on handpump. Food is served during all sessions and families are welcome at lunch and early evening until 8.30pm (unless in restaurant).

There is a large garden area to the rear of the pub. Throughout the Summer, there are several functions which raise considerable funds for charities. The Knot is used to ramblers calling and you can be assured of a welcome at this well kept pub. Opening hours are from 11 until 3pm at lunchtimes and from 6pm in the evening on Mondays to Saturdays. Usual Sunday hours.

*The Knot Inn, with Rushton's old railway station on the right*

## The Crown, Rushton Spencer (0260) 226231

The Crown is a little way out of the village on the Congleton Road, a short diversion from the ramble from Rushton Church. At the lane turn left for a 5 minute walk to the pub. The pub retains a front bar and two other rooms, one of which is away from the bar and suitable for families.

The Crown has Theakstons Best Bitter, XB, Youngers IPA and a guest beer on hand-pull and so the rambler has a choice of brews from Scottish and Newcastle here. The smells from the kitchen are delicious as the pub specialises in Greek food,served until 2.30pm at lunchtimes and 9.30pm in the evening. Opening times are noon until 3pm and from 6pm in the evening on Mondays to Saturdays. Sunday hours and standard. There is a garden area to the side of the pub by the car park. This was evidently the site of public executions in previous centuries and the locals say that ghosts are still seen in the vicinity.

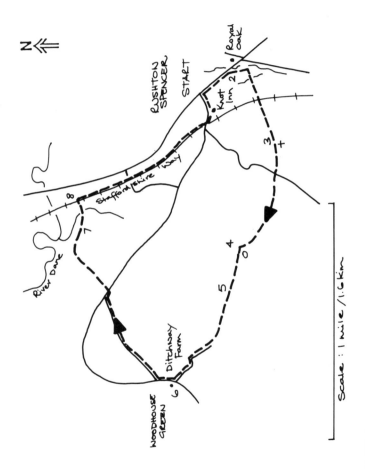

## Rushton Spencer

The border village of Rushton Spencer is surrounded by attractive walking country. It is the meeting point of the Gritstone Trail running through the Western Peakland to Lyme Park near Stockport and The Staffordshire Way. A canal feeder flows from the River Dane through Rushton Spencer to Rudyard and attracts grey herons and other birds. Rushton Church, standing aloof from the village, has been described as the "church in the wilderness", reflecting its distance from the settlement. Dating from medieval times, this little church has been restored throughout the 17th and 19th centuries. Much of the woodwork, however, is traditional and the simplicity of the structure is very appealing.

# The Walk

(1) Turn right from the entrance to the Knot Inn to walk up to the main road. Go right and continue along the pavement to a point just before the feeder canal emerges from under the road. The Royal Oak pub is to the left on the opposite side of the road.

(2) Go through a small gate here on the right. A well-trodden path follows the feeder at first but then turns right beneath the spread of a large tree and crosses to another gate. Once through, continue ahead to walk over the old railway bridge, the track-bed now being the route of the Staffordshire Way. Walk towards the church, cross a stile by a gateway and then climb up to a stile which leads into the churchyard.

(3) Walk up the steps and pass to the left of this beautiful place of worship. Go through the gateway and ahead along the drive to a narrow lane. Cross the stile (not much of one) on the other side of the road. Walk ahead in the field, with a stream bed to the right. Head for a point to the left of two oak trees in the far hedge. Cross the boundary. In the next large field bear slightly right. There is no clear landmark to aim for except a collection of bushes which lines a pond.

(4) The path leads to the right of this, through scrub and re-colonising marsh plants where the water has receded in recent years. Wade through the long grass to stile. Cross it and bear slightly left across the field to join a hedge on the left. Follow this up a bank to cross a concrete footbridge and stile, then proceed ahead in the next field.

(5) You will see the roof of a house as you go over the remains of another stile by a gateway. Continue ahead to walk the entire length of the next field as it narrows to a corner where holly and hazel conspire to hide a stile which leads to a track. This stile is awkward, so take care. Join the road and follow this as it climbs up by Ditchway Farm.

(6) At the junction turn right in the hamlet of Woodhouse Green, no more than a few houses and farms. Turn right again at the next junction by the telephone kiosk. This road drops to another junction in approximately one quarter of a mile. There is a barn on the left and a house on the right. Go right but then immediately left through a gap-stile into a pasture where a deep gully cuts down on the left. Keep ahead down the bank to join a hedge at the corner by a tree. Then continue with a hedge to the right. The path becomes a track which drops down a to a bluff above the River Dane.

(7) At the top of the bluff go right by the waymark and follow the bluff as it curves left and then right with a tree lined tributary stream below. This soon comes to a stile and stone footbridge. Cross these and go ahead to a stile which marks the junction between The Gritstone Trail and Staffordshire Way.

(8) Climb the embankment and turn right to walk along the track-bed about half a mile to the road by the old railway station (now a private residence) and the Knot Inn on the left.

*The Church, Rushton*

Explore the countryside with Sigma!. We have a wide selection of guides to individual towns from Buxton to Lancaster, plus outdoor activities centred on walking and cycling in the great outdoors throughout England and Wales. Here are some recent highlights:

**PEAK DISTRICT DIARY** - Roger Redfern
An evocative book, celebrating the glorious countryside of the Peak District. The book is based on Roger's popular column in *The Guardian* newspaper and is profusely illustrated with stunning photographs. *£6.95*

**I REMAIN, YOUR SON JACK** - J. C. Morten (edited by Sheila Morten)
A collection of almost 200 letters, as featured on BBC TV, telling the moving story of a young soldier in the First World War. Profusely illustrated with contemporary photographs. *£8.95*

There are many books for outdoor people in our catalogue, including:

**HERITAGE WALKS IN THE PEAK DISTRICT**
**- Clive Price**

**EAST CHESHIRE WALKS**
**- Graham Beech**

**WEST CHESHIRE WALKS**
**- Jen Darling**

**WEST PENNINE WALKS**
**- Mike Cresswell**

**NEWARK AND SHERWOOD RAMBLES**
**- Malcolm McKenzie**

**RAMBLES AROUND MANCHESTER**
**- Mike Cresswell**

**WESTERN LAKELAND RAMBLES**
**- Gordon Brown**

**WELSH WALKS: Dolgellau and the Cambrian Coast**
**- Laurence Main and Morag Perrott**

**WELSH WALKS: Aberystwyth and District**
**- Laurence Main and Morag Perrott**

**Cycling in The Cotswolds**
**– Stephen Hill**

**OFF-BEAT CYCLING IN THE PEAK DISTRICT**
**- Clive Smith**